RECORDED VERSIONS
GUITAR

AUTHENTIC TRANSCRIPTIONS
WITH NOTES AND TABLATURE

THE OZZMAN COM

ISBN 0-634-01365-3

HAL•LEONARD®
CORPORATION

7777 W. BLUEMOUND RD. P.O. BOX 13819 MILWAUKEE, WI 53213

Visit Hal Leonard Online at
www.halleonard.com

Black Sabbath

Words and Music by Frank Iommi, John Osbourne, William Ward and Terence Butler

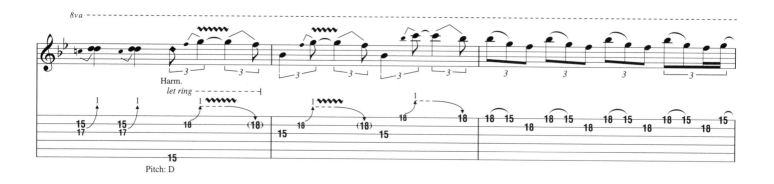

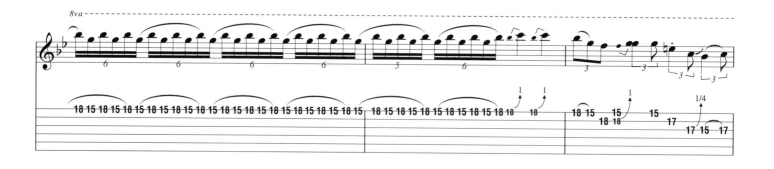

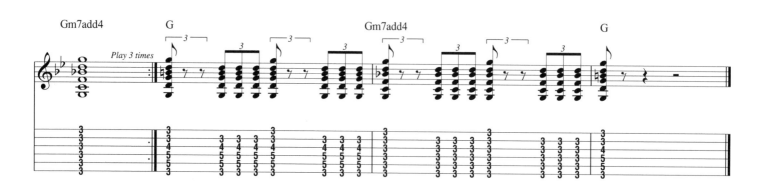

War Pigs
(Interpolating Luke's Wall)

Words and Music by Frank Iommi, John Osbourne, William Ward and Terence Butler

Verse

1. Witch - es gath - er at black mass - es. Bod - ies burn - ing in red ash -
2. On the scene a priest ap - pears, sin - ners fall - ing at his

- es. On the hill, the church in ru - ins
knees. Sa - tan sends our fu - ner - al py - res,

is the scene of e - vil do - in'. It's the place for all bad
casts the priest in - to the fi - re.

Fill 1

End Fill 1

sin - ners. Watch them eat - ing dead rat din - ners.

Gtr. 1: w/ Rhy. Fig. 1 (2 times)

I guess it's the same wher - ev - er you may go. Oh, Lord, yeah!

Fill 2
Gtr. 1

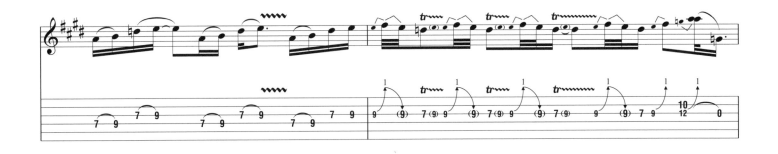

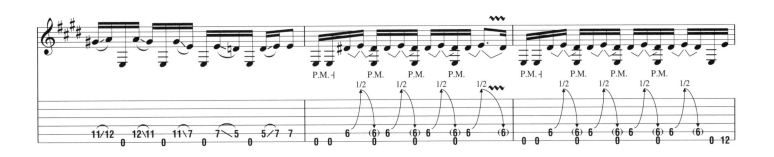

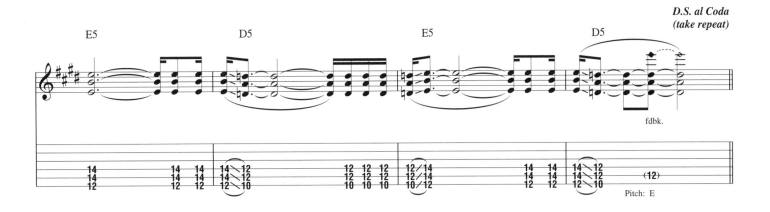

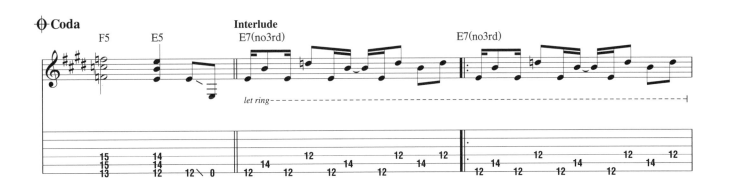

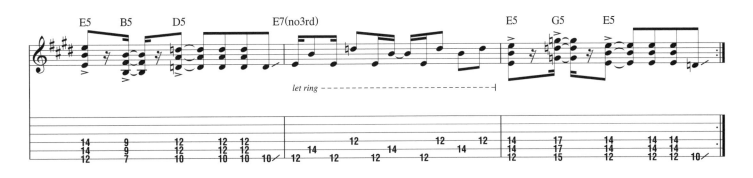

Goodbye to Romance

**Words and Music by John Osbourne,
Robert Daisley and Randy Rhoads**

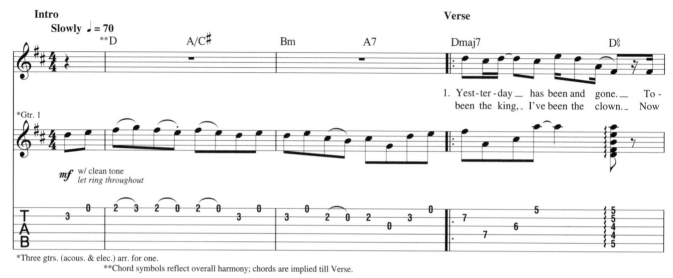

*Three gtrs. (acous. & elec.) arr. for one.
**Chord symbols reflect overall harmony; chords are implied till Verse.

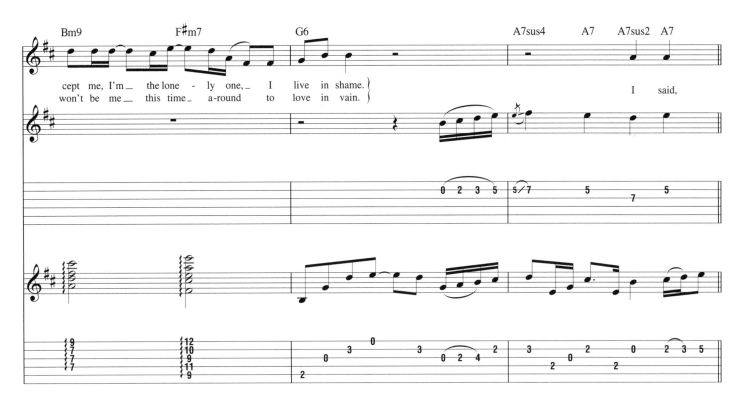

cept me, I'm _ the lone - ly one, _ I live in shame.
won't be me _ this time _ a-round to love in vain.

I said,

Chorus
3rd time, Gtr. 3: w/ Fill 1

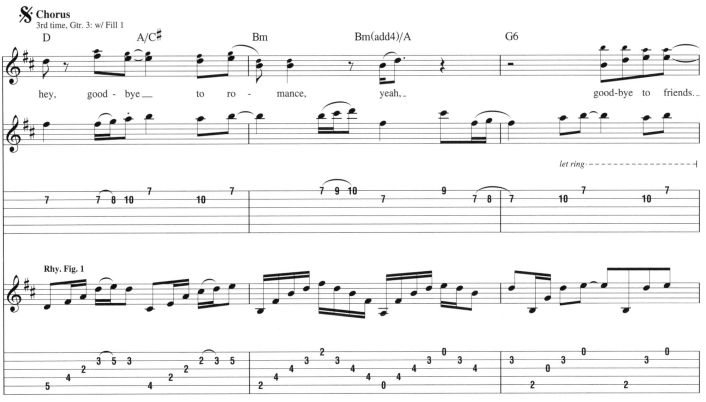

hey, good-bye _ to ro - mance, yeah, _ good-bye to friends. _

Rhy. Fig. 1

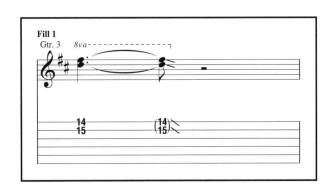

Fill 1
Gtr. 3

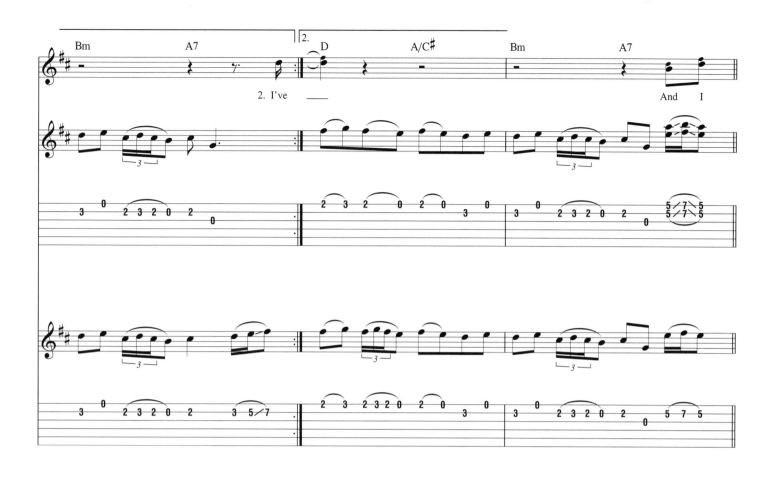

2. I've ____

And I

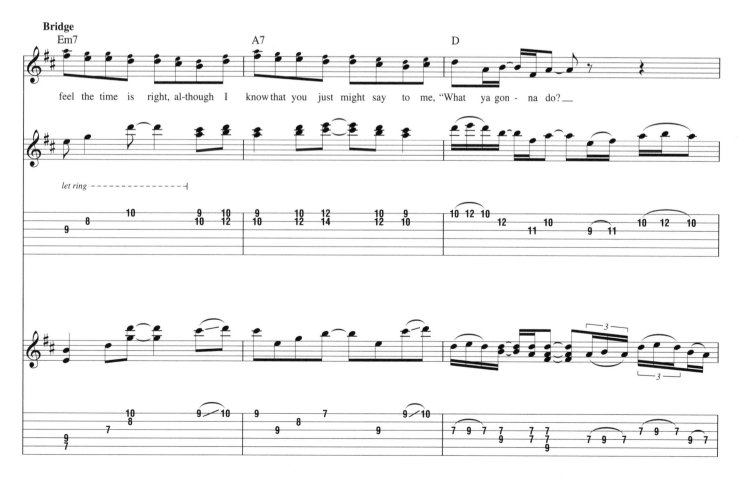

Bridge

feel the time is right, al-though I know that you just might say to me, "What ya gon - na do? ____

let ring - - - - - - - - - -

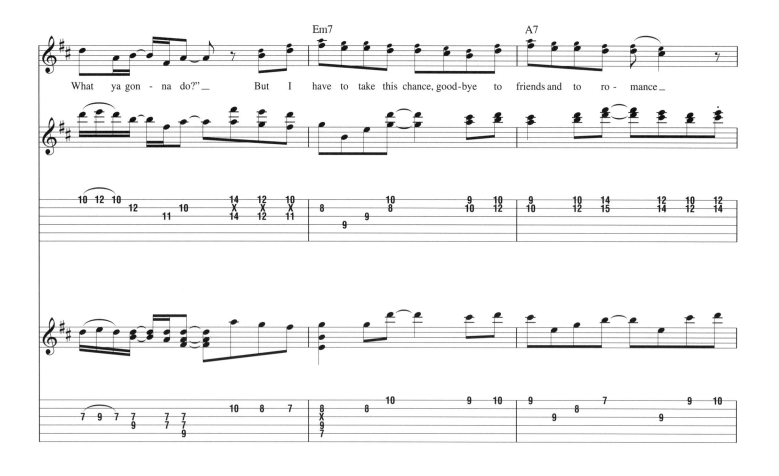

What ya gon - na do?"__ But I have to take this chance, good-bye to friends and to ro - mance__

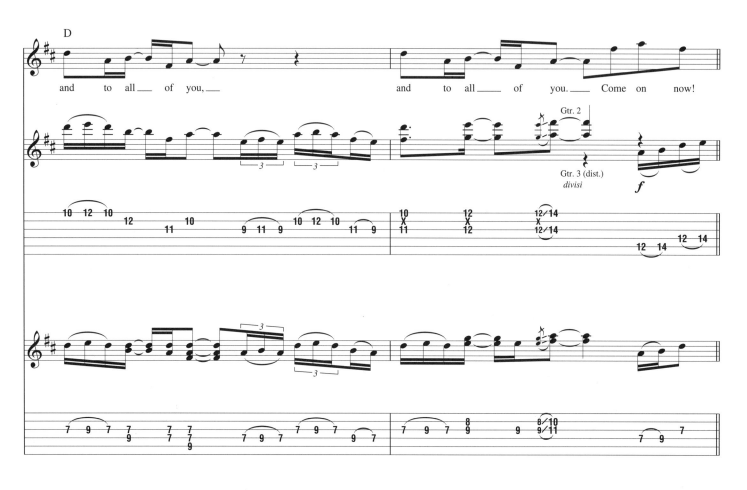

and to all__ of you,__ and to all__ of you.__ Come on now!

Gtr. 2

Gtr. 3 (dist.)
divisi

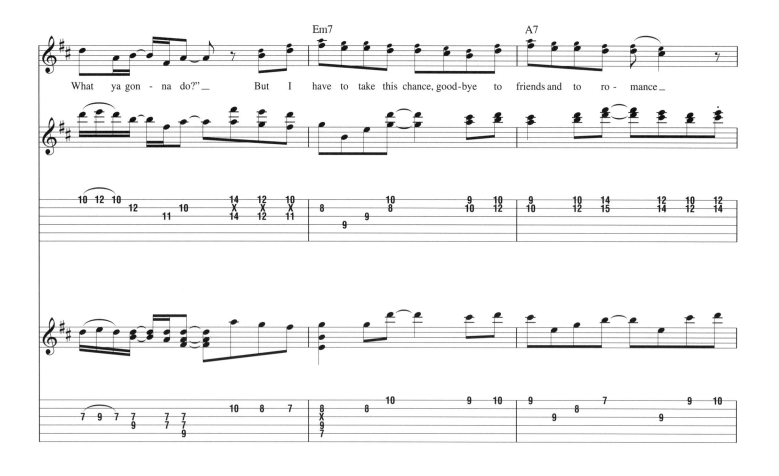

Guitar Solo
Gtr. 1: w/ Rhy. Fig. 1 (2 times)
Gtr. 2 tacet

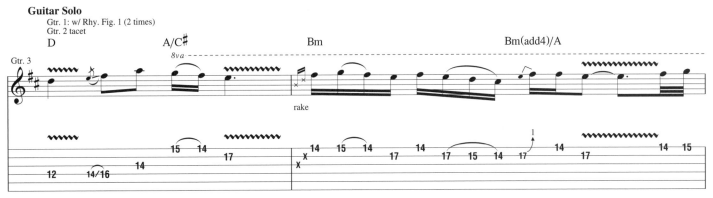

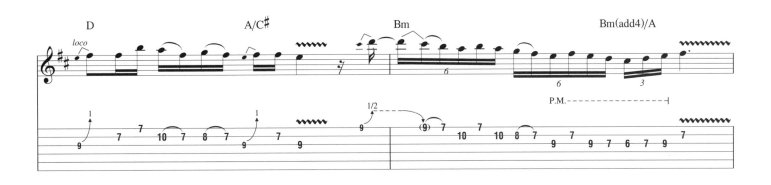

D.S. al Coda 1

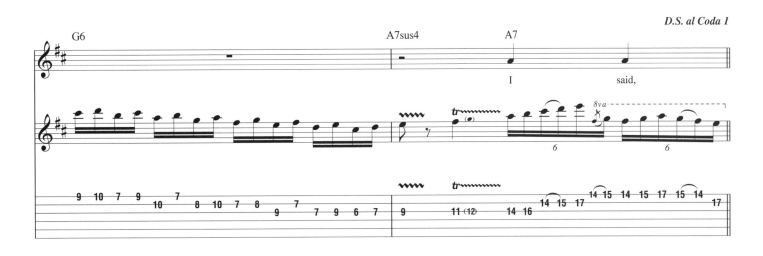

Coda 1

Gtr. 2: w/ Rhy. Fill 2

we'll _ meet in the end. _

*Gtrs. 3 & 4 (dist.)

mf

*Composite arrangement

Gtr. 1

Bridge

Gtr. 1: w/ Rhy. Fig. 1 (2 times)

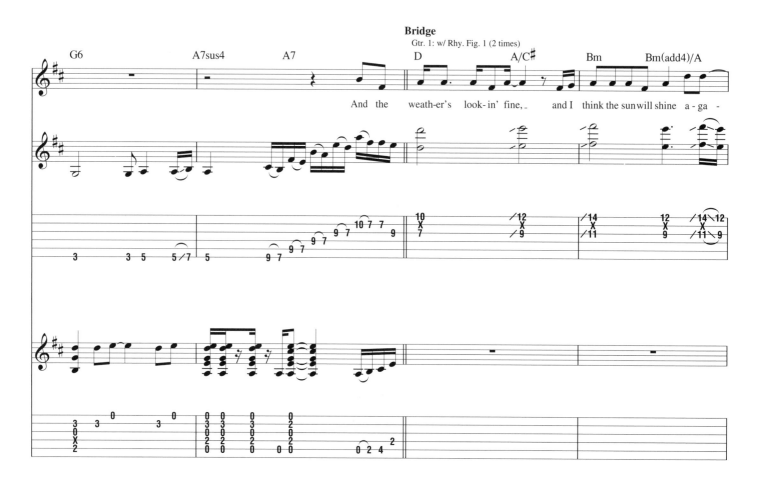

And the weath-er's look-in' fine, _ and I think the sun will shine a - ga -

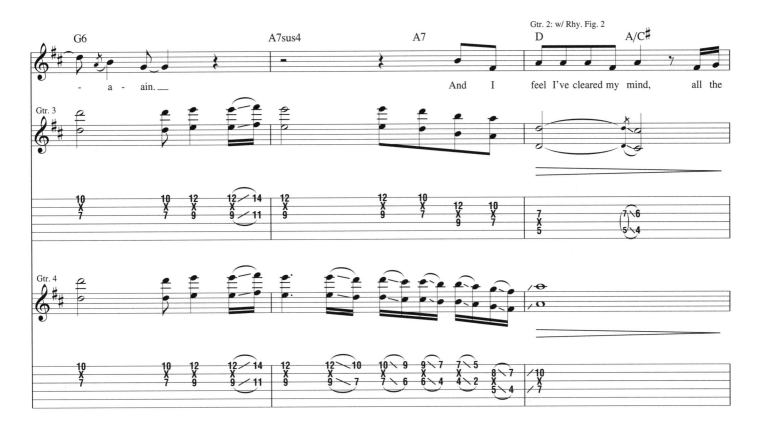

D.S. al Coda 2

past is left be- hind a- ga - a- ain. ___ I said,

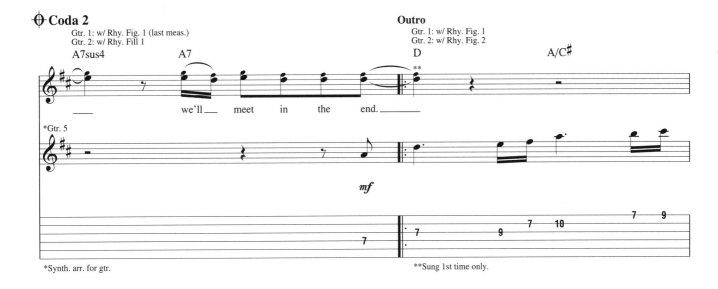

$\oplus$ **Coda 2**

Gtr. 1: w/ Rhy. Fig. 1 (last meas.)
Gtr. 2: w/ Rhy. Fill 1

Outro

Gtr. 1: w/ Rhy. Fig. 1
Gtr. 2: w/ Rhy. Fig. 2

we'll ___ meet in the end. ___

*Gtr. 5

mf

*Synth. arr. for gtr.

**Sung 1st time only.

Repeat and fade

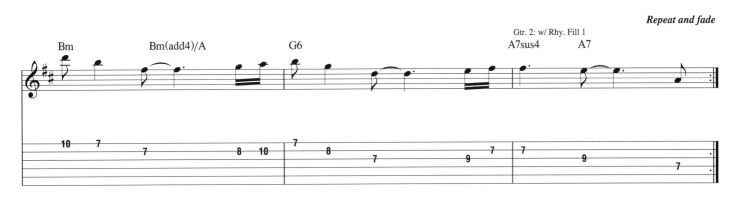

Crazy Train

Words and Music by Ozzy Osbourne, Randy Rhoads and Bob Daisley

Gtr. 1: w/ Fill 3, 3rd time, see previous page

Gtr. 1: w/ Fill 1, 2nd time

go-ing off ___ the rails ___ on a cra-zy train. ___

I'm go-ing off ___ the rails ___ on a cra-zy train. ___

*Harm.

*Harm.

*Located between 1st and 2nd frets.

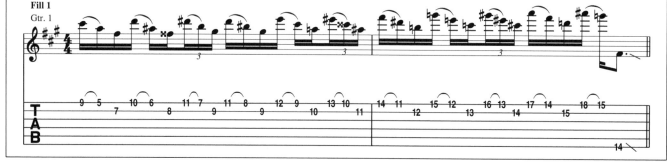

Fill 1
Gtr. 1

Guitar Solo

24

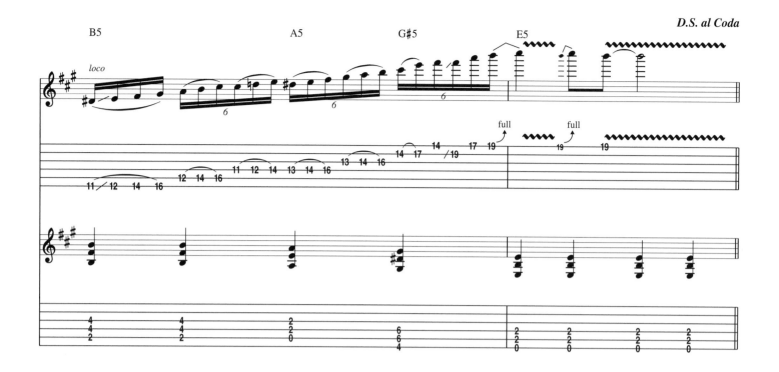

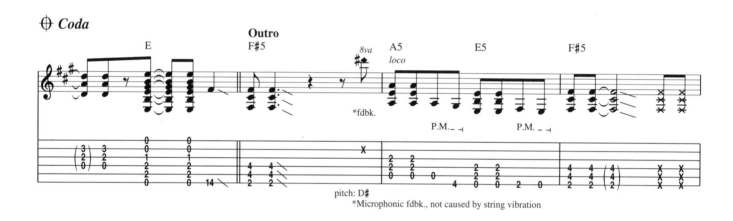

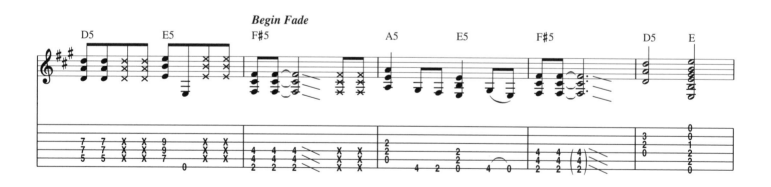

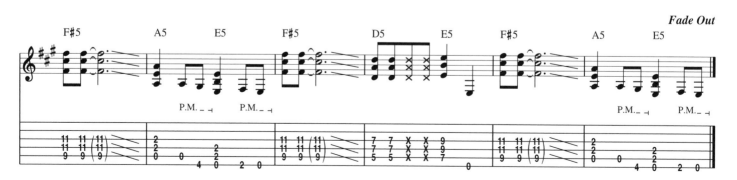

Mr. Crowley

Words and Music by Ozzy Osbourne, Randy Rhoads and Bob Daisley

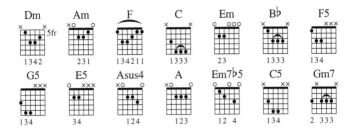

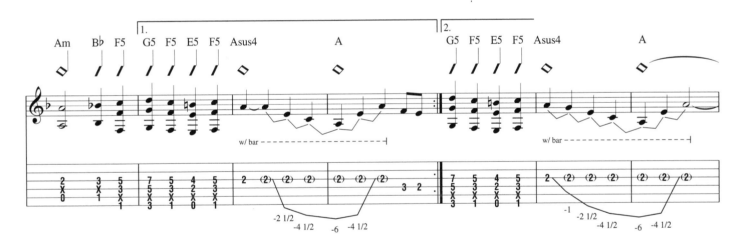

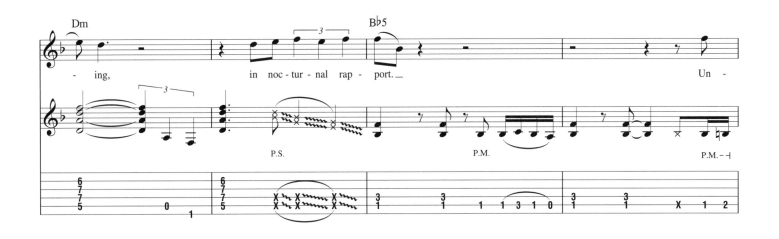

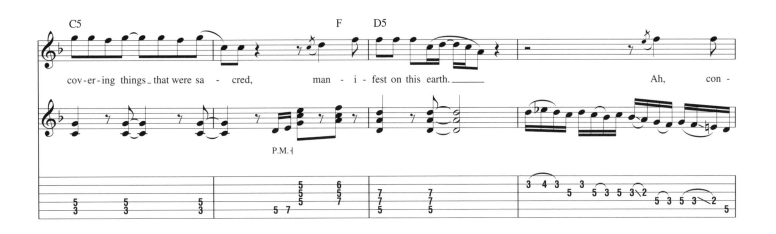

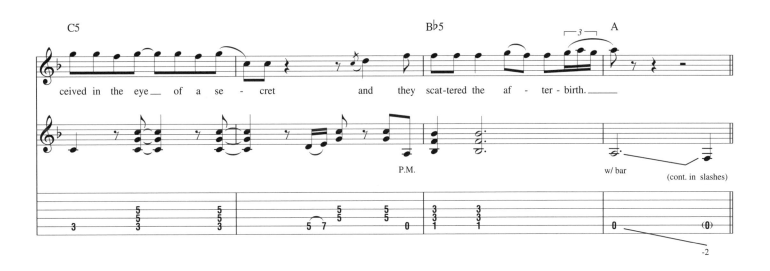

Guitar Solo

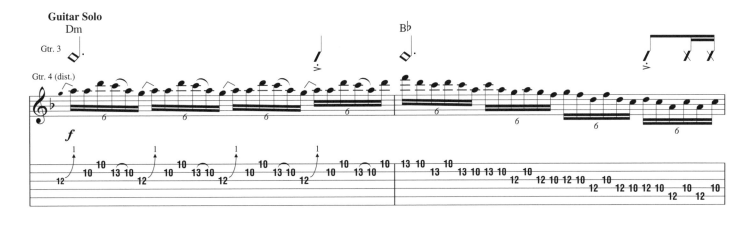

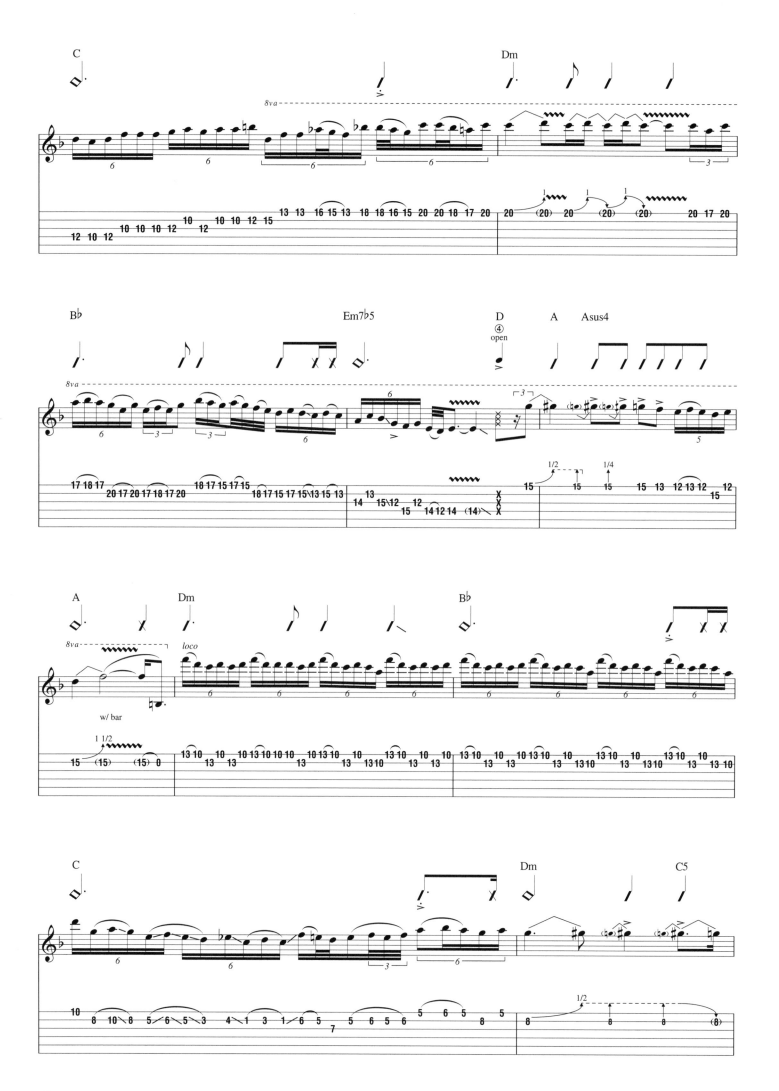

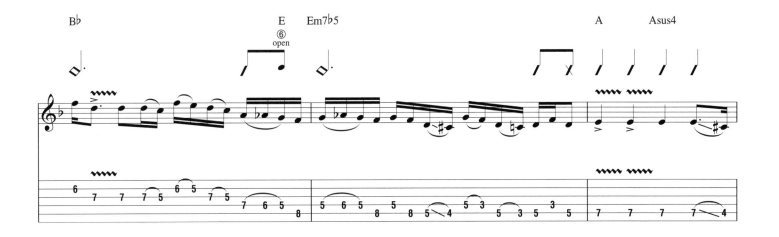

Verse
Gtr. 4 tacet

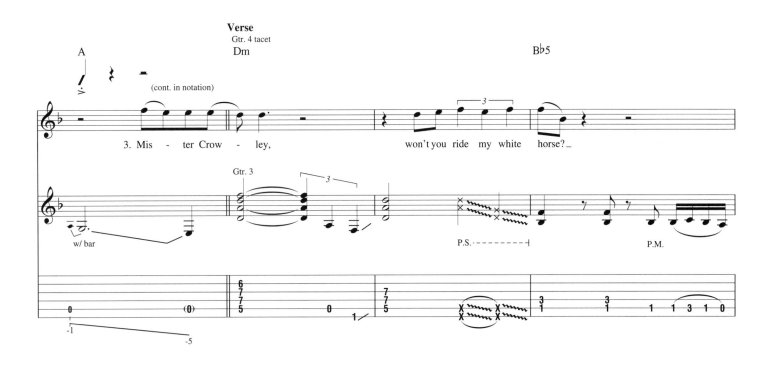

3. Mis - ter Crow - ley, won't you ride my white horse?_

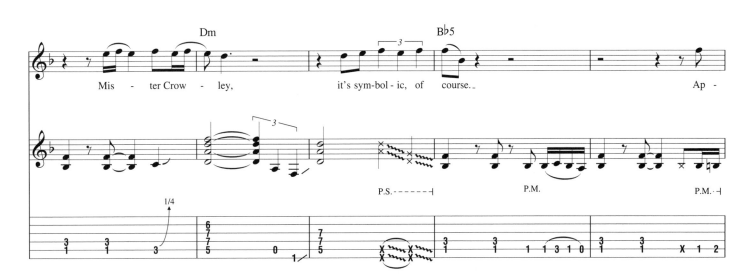

Mis - ter Crow - ley, it's sym-bol - ic, of course._ Ap -

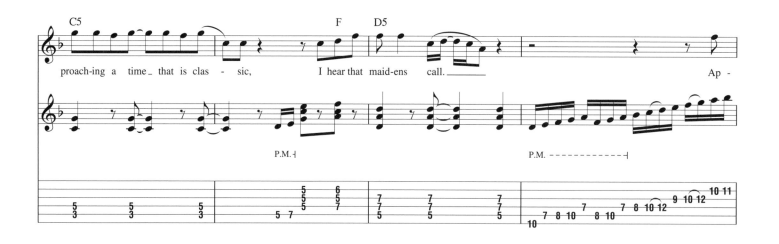

proach-ing a time _ that is clas - sic,   I hear that maid-ens call. _   Ap -

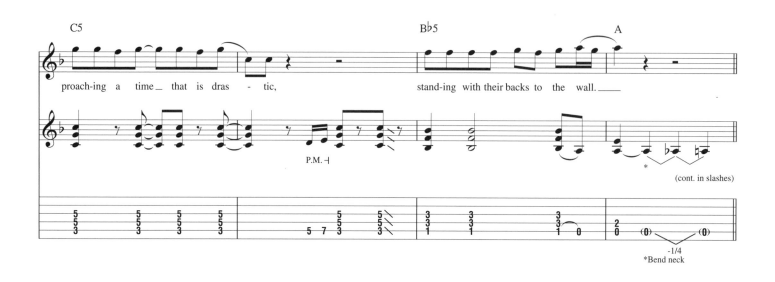

proach-ing a time _ that is dras - tic,   stand-ing with their backs to the wall. _

(cont. in slashes)

-1/4
*Bend neck

Interlude

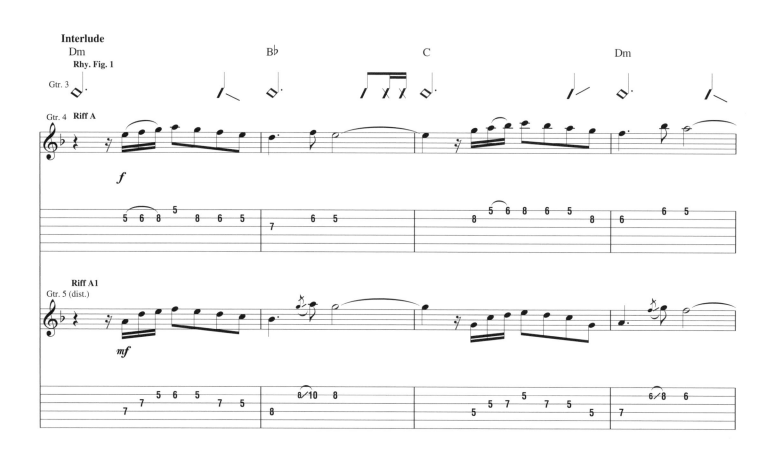

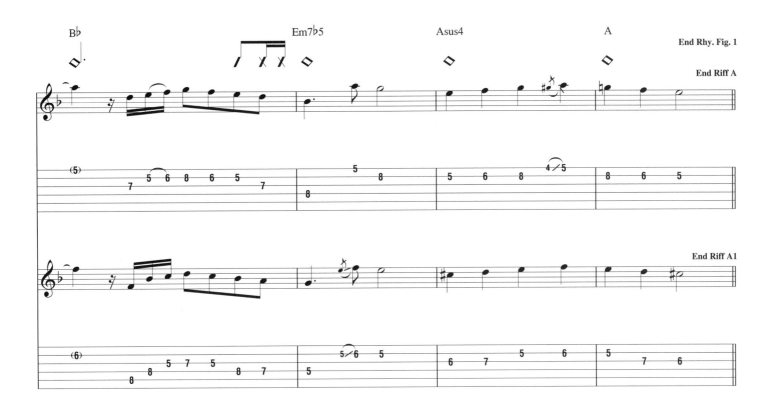

Bridge

Gtr. 3: w/ Rhy. Fig. 1
Gtrs. 4 & 5: w/ Riffs A & A1

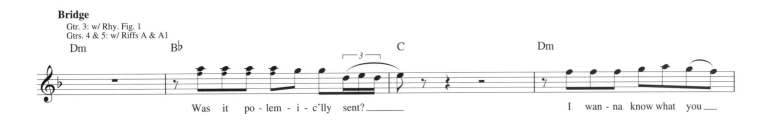

Was it po - lem - i - c'lly sent?_____ I wan - na know what you ___

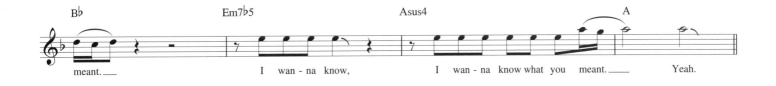

meant. ___ I wan - na know, I wan - na know what you meant. ___ Yeah.

Outro - Guitar Solo

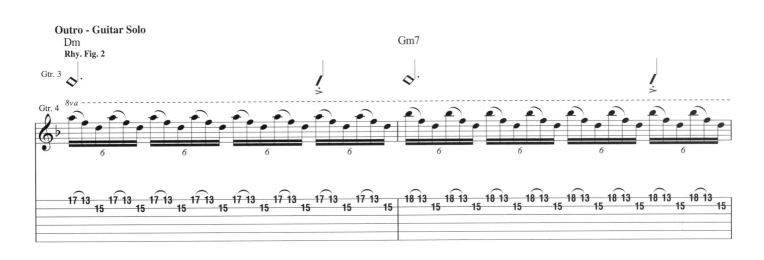

Over the Mountain

**Words and Music by Ozzy Osbourne, Randy Rhoads,
Bob Daisley and Lee Kerslake**

*Chord symbols reflect basic harmony.

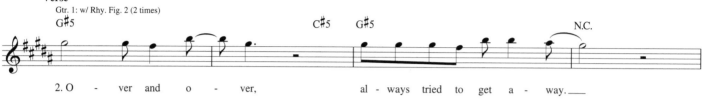

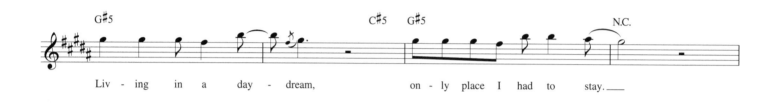

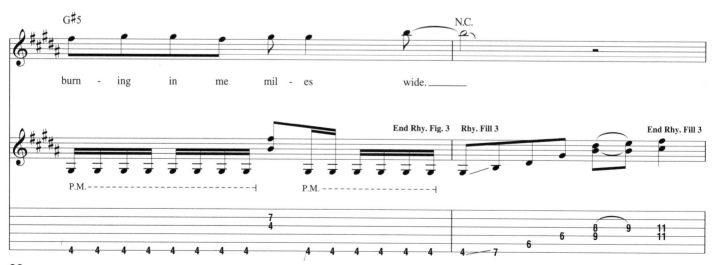

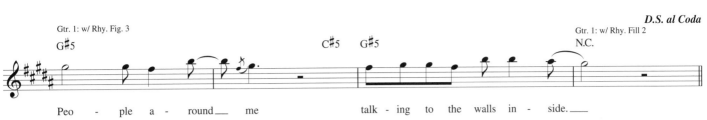

Peo - ple a - round___ me   talk - ing to the walls in - side.___

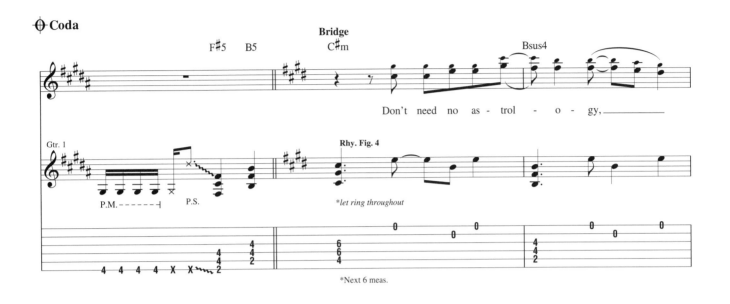

Don't need no as - trol - o - gy,___

it's in - side of you___ and___ me.___   You don't need a tick -

- et to fly___ with me,___   I'm   free,___   yeah.

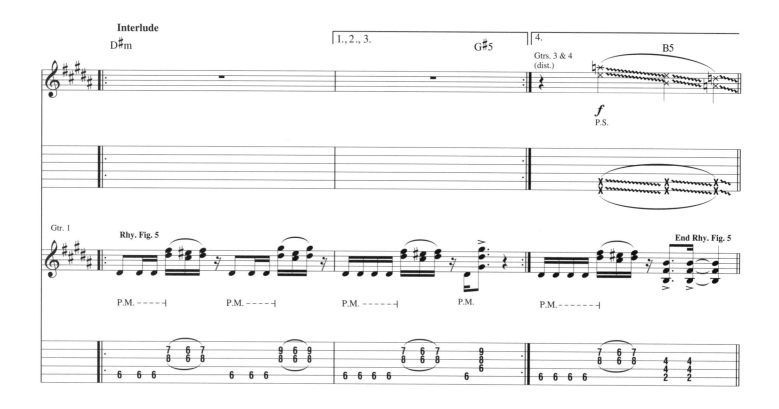

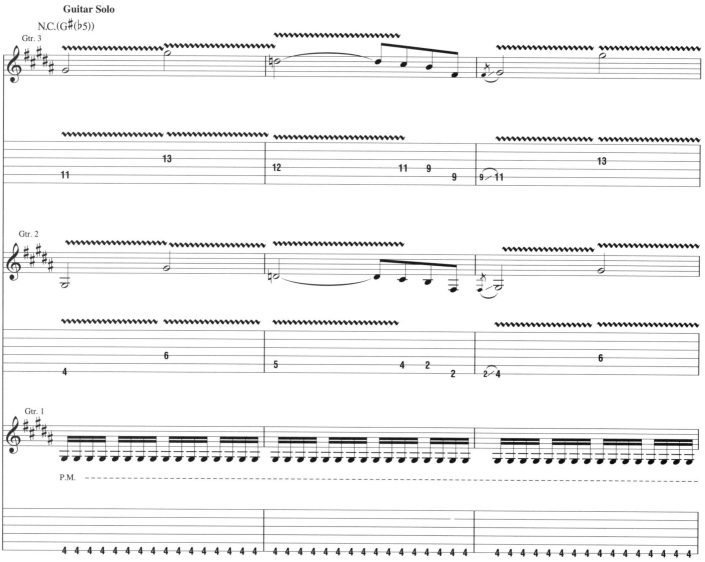

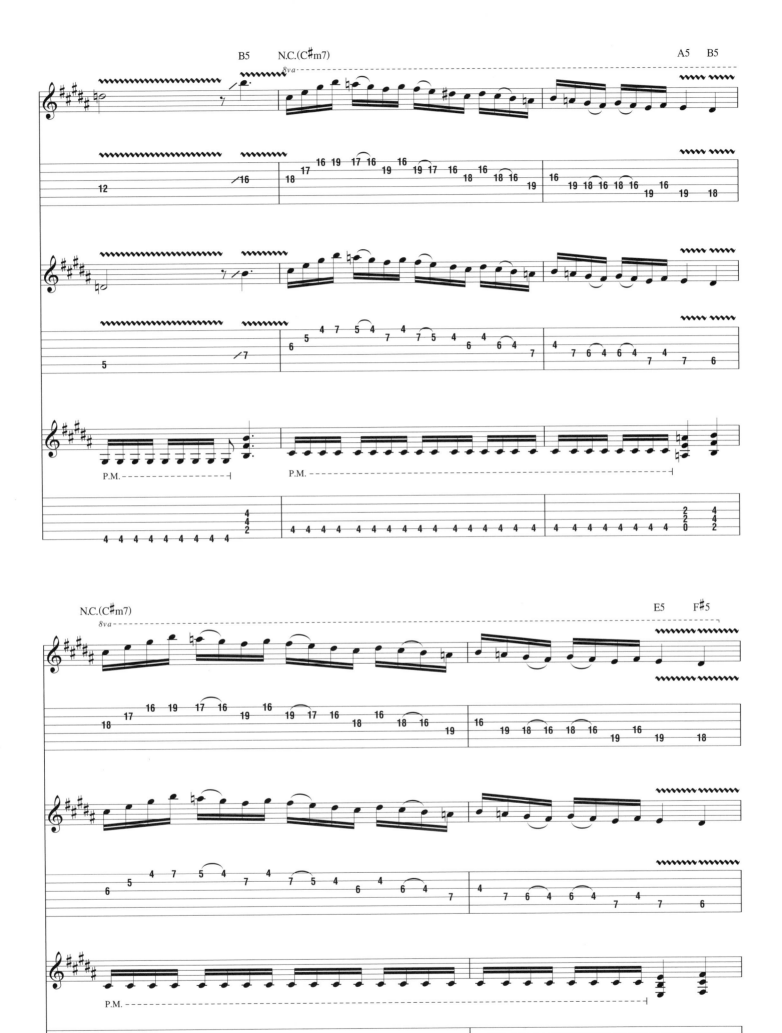

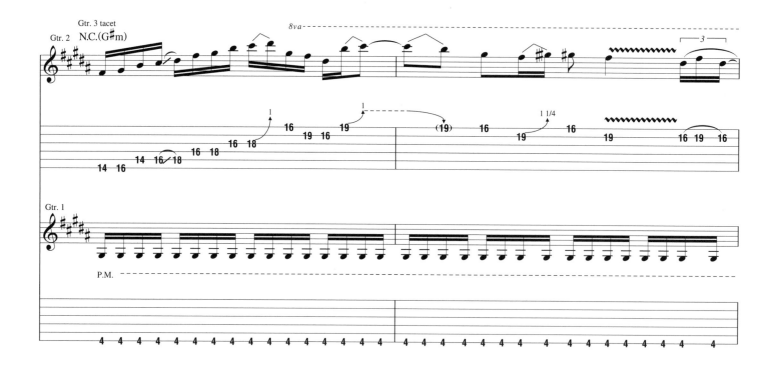

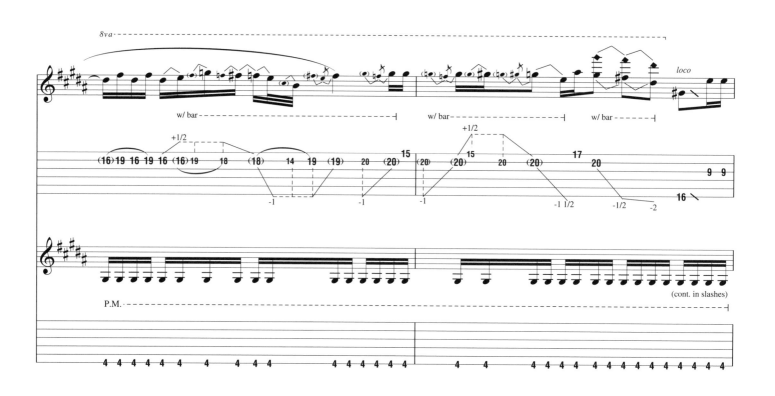

Interlude

Gtr. 1: w/ Rhy. Fig. 1 (1 1/2 times)
Gtr. 2 tacet

Gtr. 1: w/ Rhy. Fill 1

E5^{type2} A5 G#5   N.C.(E5) A5 G#5   N.C.(E5) (F#5)

Verse

Gtr. 1: w/ Rhy. Fig. 2 (2 times)

G#5   C#5 G#5   N.C.

3. O - ver and un - der,   in be - tween the ups and   downs.

G#5   C#5 G#5   N.C.

Mind   on a car - pet _____ mag - ic ride goes round and   round.

Paranoid

**Words and Music by Anthony Iommi, John Osbourne,
William Ward and Terence Butler**

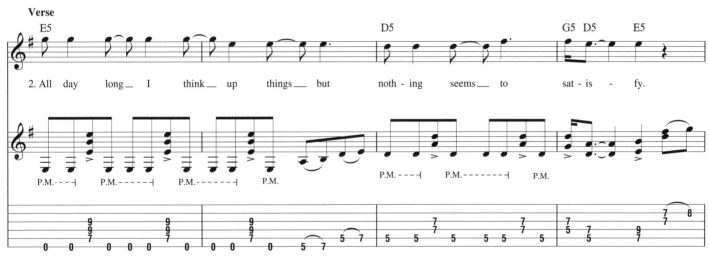

Bridge

Can you help___ me?   Oc - cu - py ___ my brain.___

Pitch: F#

___   Oh,___   yeah.___   *Come on. I want to see you clap your hands.*

Interlude

Verse

3. I need some - one to ___ show me ___ the things ___ in life ___ that

Guitar Solo

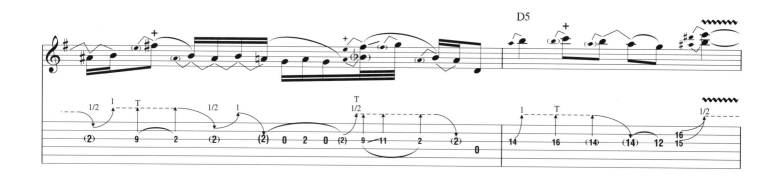

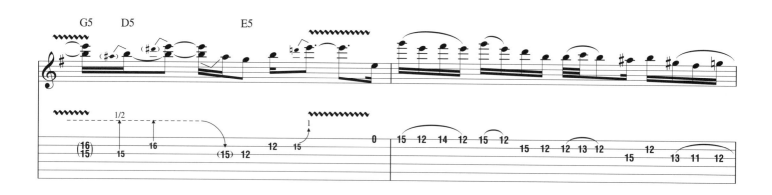

Let me see your hands now.

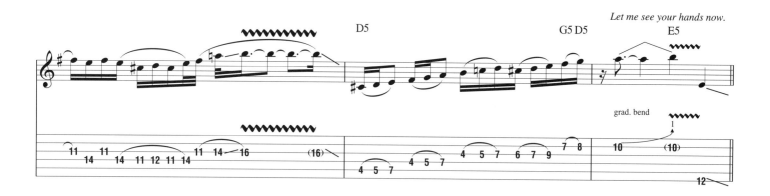

Interlude

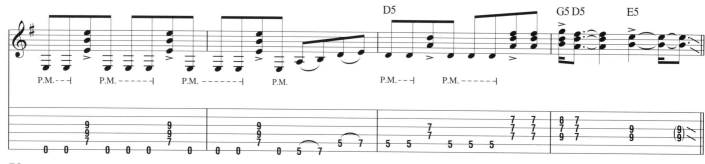

Verse

4. Make a joke ___ and I ___ will sigh, ___ and you will laugh, ___ and

I will ___ cry. Hap - pi - ness ___ I can - not feel, ___ and love ___

Pitch: G♯

___ to me ___ is so un - real.

* Bend neck

Come on. ___

Harm.

Pitch: G

** Using a guitar with Les Paul style electronics, set lead volume to 0 and rhythm volume to 10. Strike the strings while the pickup selector switch is in the lead position, then flip the switch in the rhythm indicated to simulate the re-attack.

Bark at the Moon

Words and Music by Ozzy Osbourne

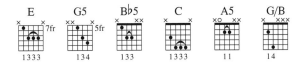

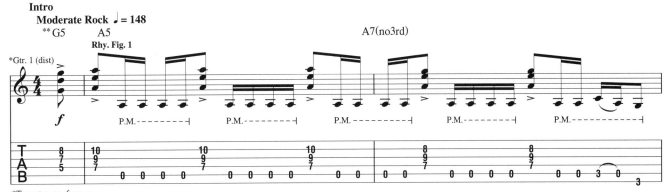

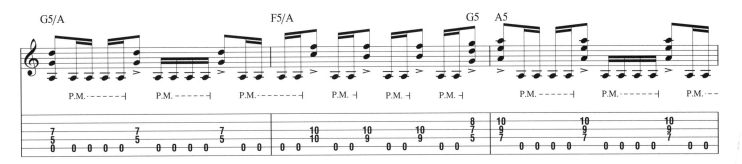

Two gtrs. arr. for one
**Chord symbols reflect basic harmony.

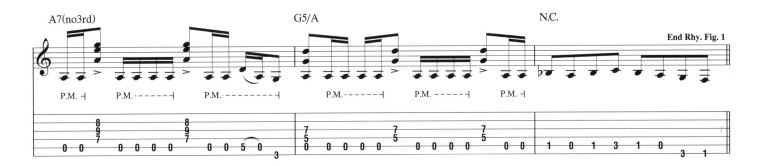

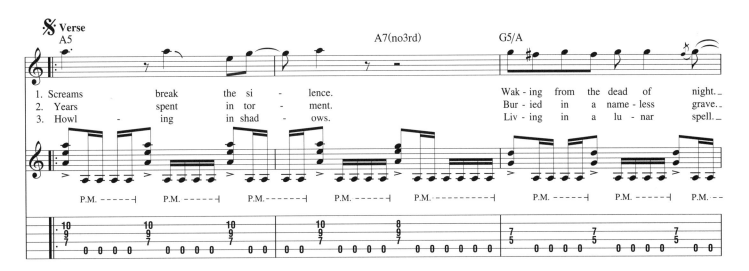

1. Screams break the si - lence.
2. Years spent in tor - ment.
3. Howl - ing in shad - ows.

Wak - ing from the dead of night.
Bur - ied in a name - less grave.
Liv - ing in a lu - nar spell.

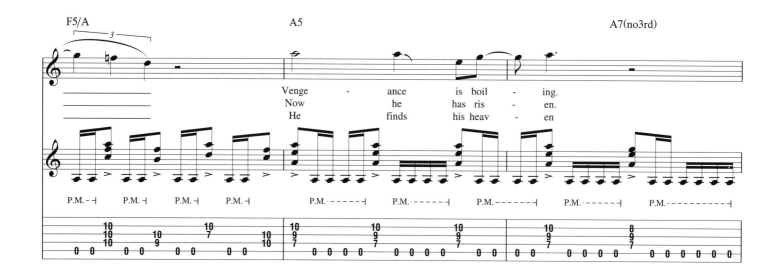

F5/A   A5   A7(no3rd)

Venge - ance is boil - ing.
Now he has ris - en.
He finds his heav - en

P.M. P.M. P.M. P.M. P.M. P.M. P.M. P.M. P.M.

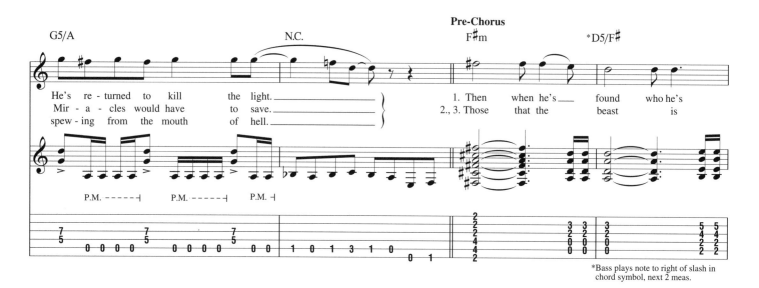

G5/A   N.C.   **Pre-Chorus**   F#m   *D5/F#

He's re - turned to kill the light. _____
Mir - a - cles would have to save. _____
spew - ing from the mouth of hell. _____

1. Then when he's ___ found who he's
2., 3. Those that the beast is

P.M. P.M. P.M.

*Bass plays note to right of slash in
chord symbol, next 2 meas.

2nd time, Gtr. 1: w/ Fill 2
3rd time, Gtr. 1: w/ Fill 3

E5/F#   N.C.(F#5)   F#m   **D5/F#

look - ing for, _____
look - ing for, _____

lis - ten in ___ awe and you'll
lis - ten in ___ awe and you'll

P.M.

**Bass plays F#.

Fill 2
Gtr. 1

P.M.

Fill 3
Gtr. 1

P.M.

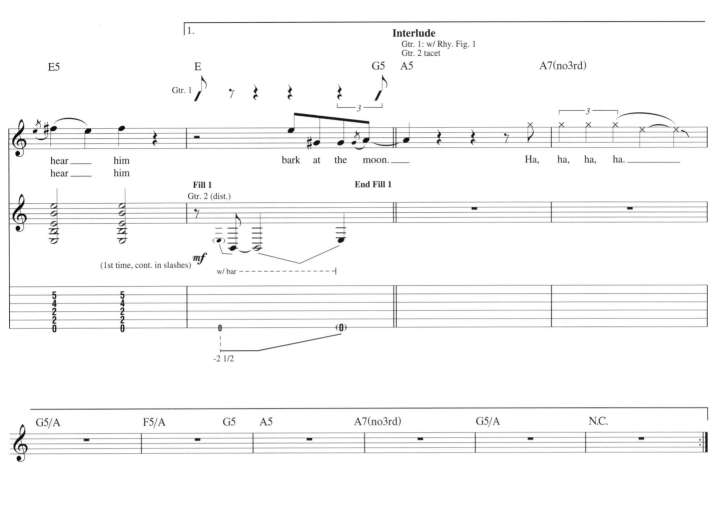

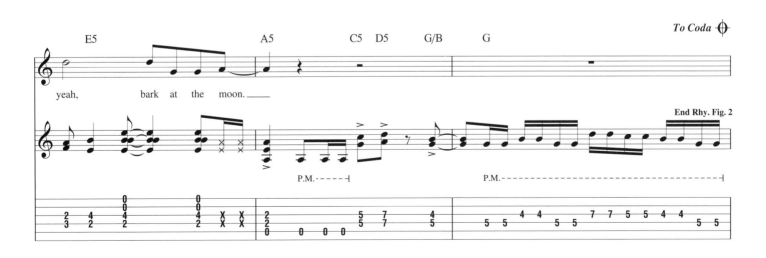

Guitar Solo
End half-time feel

Ooh yeah, ba - by.

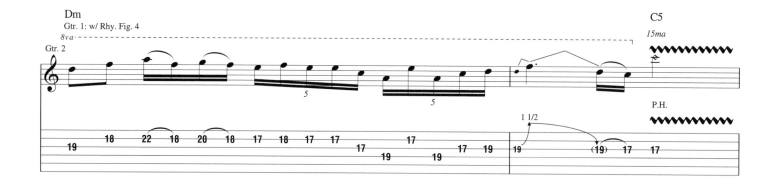

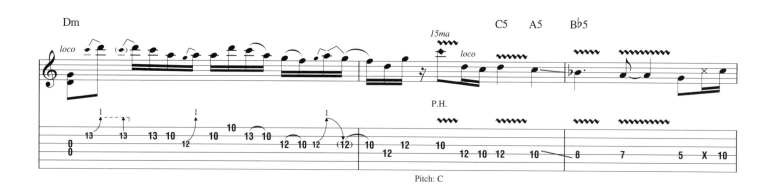

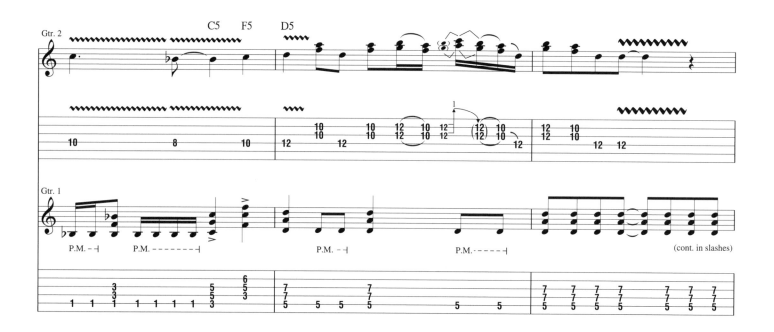

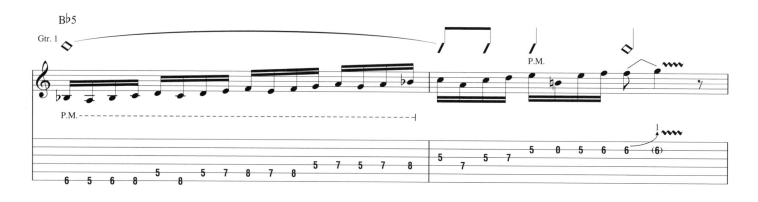

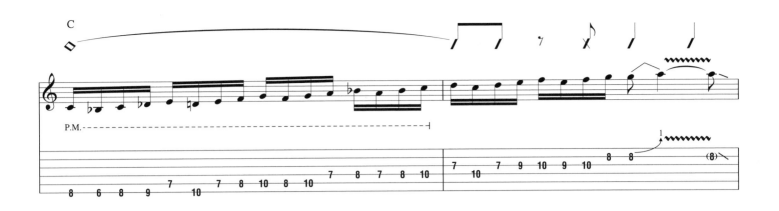

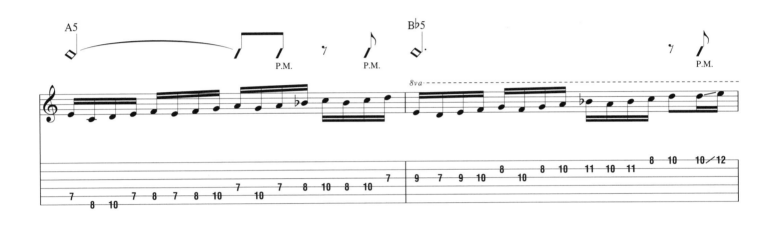

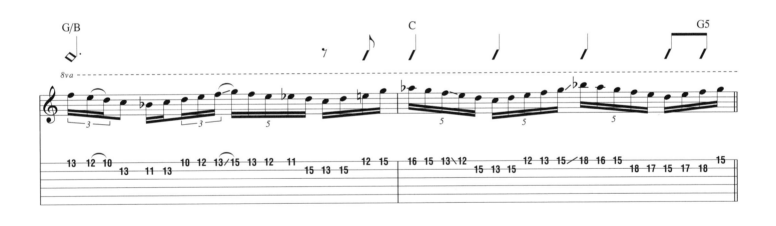

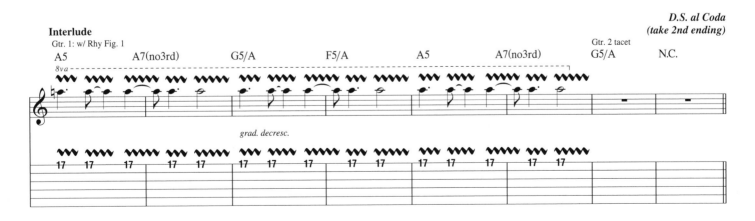

Shot in the Dark

Words and Music by Ozzy Osbourne and Phil Soussan

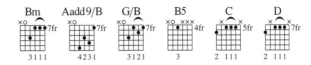

Tuning:
(low to high) F-B♭-D♭-G♭-B♭-E♭

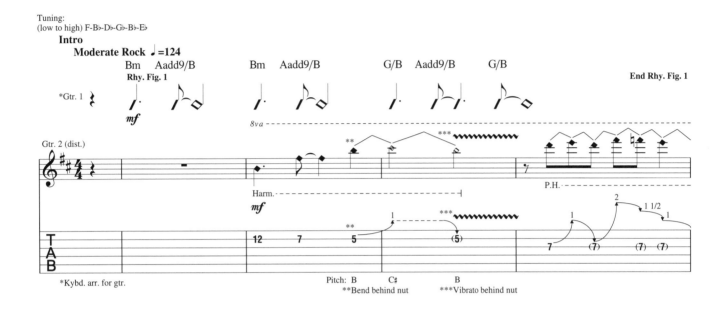

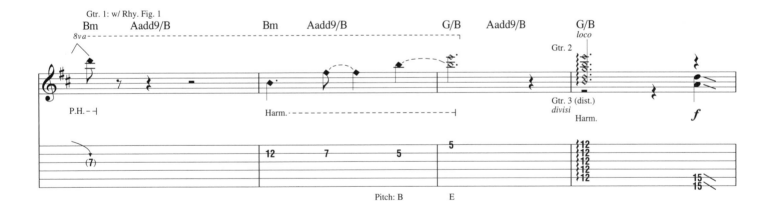

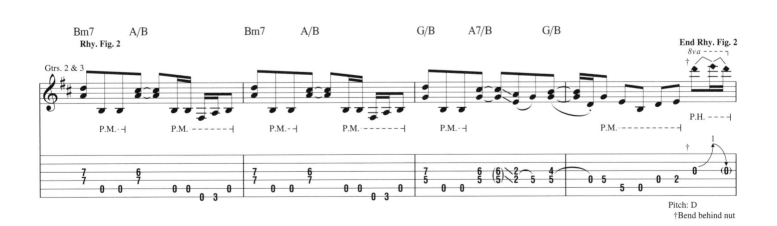

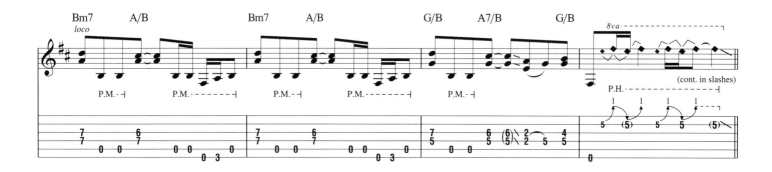

Verse

1. Out on the street, I'm stalk-ing the night,____
2. Taught by the pow-ers that preach o-ver me,____

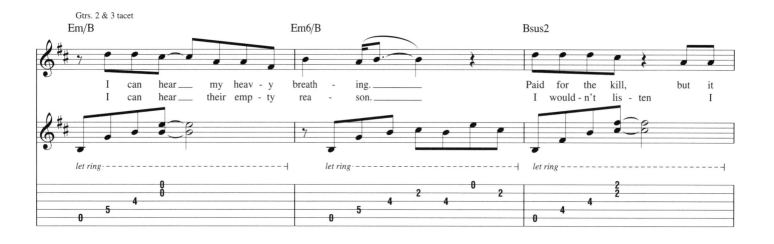

I can hear____ my heav-y breath-ing.____ Paid for the kill, but it
I can hear____ their emp-ty rea-son.____ I would-n't lis-ten I

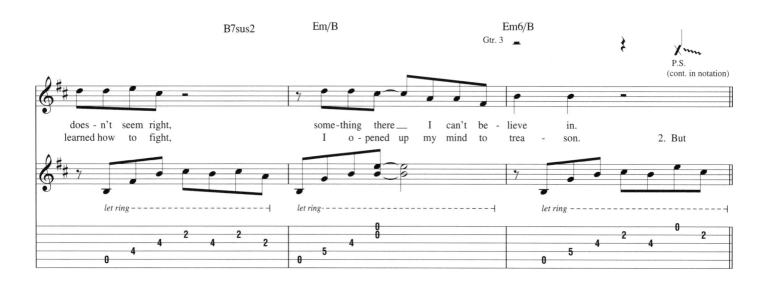

does-n't seem right, some-thing there____ I can't be-lieve in.
learned how to fight, I o-pened up my mind to trea-son. 2. But

Pre-Chorus

3rd time, Gtr. 2: w/ Fill 2

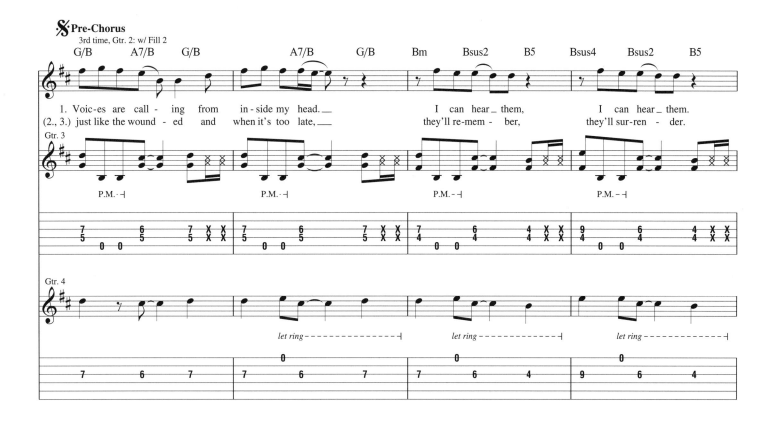

1. Voic-es are call - ing from in - side my head. ___ I can hear ___ them, I can hear ___ them.

(2., 3.) just like the wound - ed and when it's too late, ___ they'll re-mem - ber, they'll sur-ren - der.

Van - ish - ing mem - 'ries of things that were said, they can't try to hurt ___ me now. ___ But a

Nev - er a care ___ for the peo - ple who hate, un - der - es - ti - mate ___ me now. ___ But a

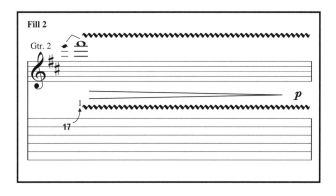

Fill 2

Guitar Solo

*Trill to higher notes by hammering and pulling off with the edge of the pick, while the left hand frets the lower notes.

Crazy Babies

Words and Music by Ozzy Osbourne, Robert Daisley, Zakk Wylde and Randy Castillo

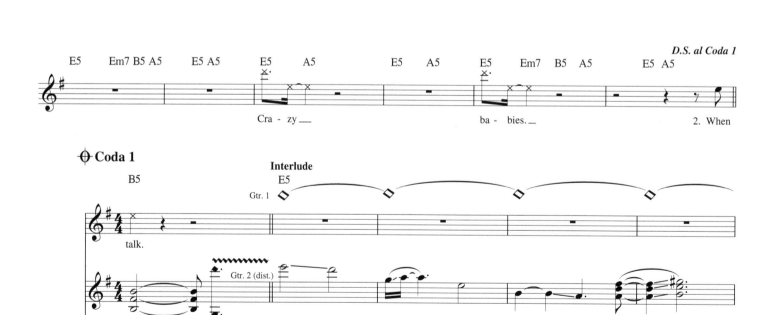

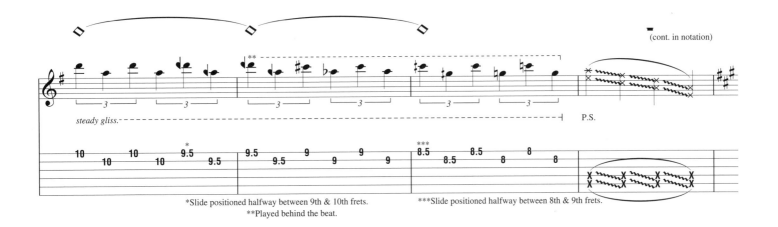

(cont. in notation)

steady gliss. --- P.S.

*Slide positioned halfway between 9th & 10th frets.
**Played behind the beat.

***Slide positioned halfway between 8th & 9th frets.

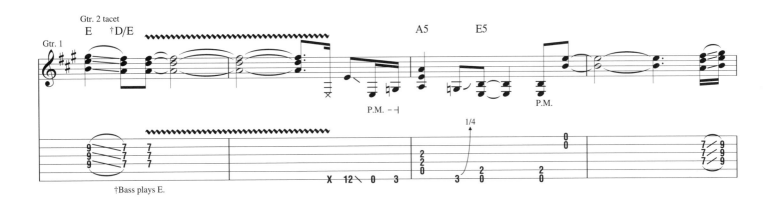

†Bass plays E.

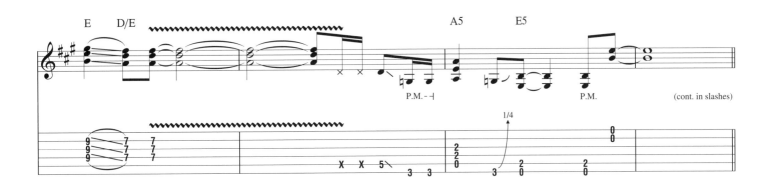

(cont. in slashes)

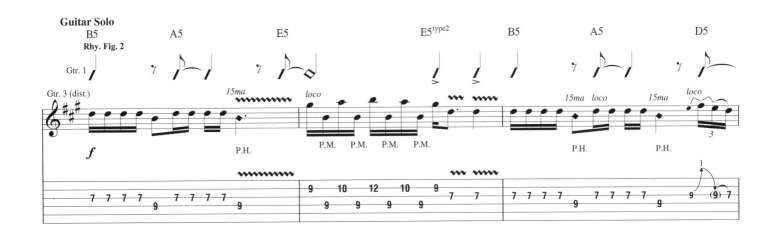

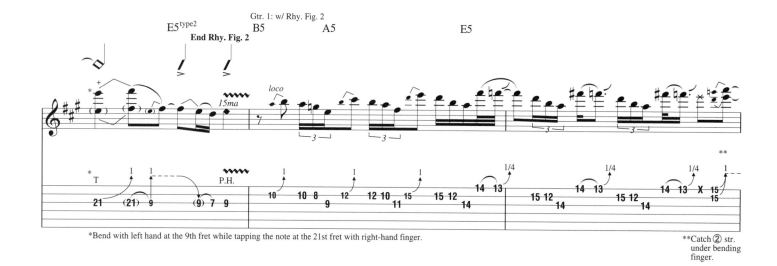

*Bend with left hand at the 9th fret while tapping the note at the 21st fret with right-hand finger.

**Catch ② str.
under bending
finger.

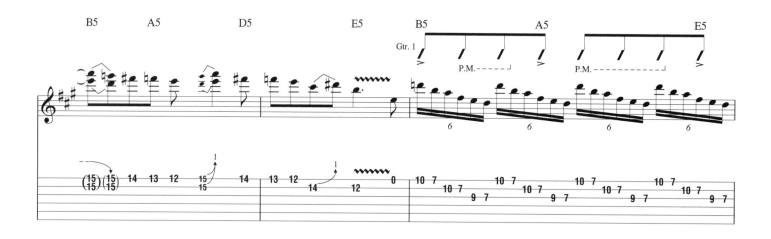

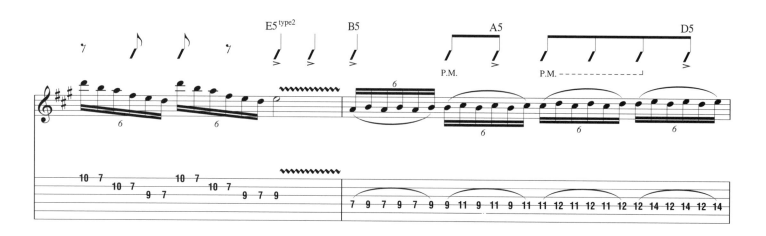

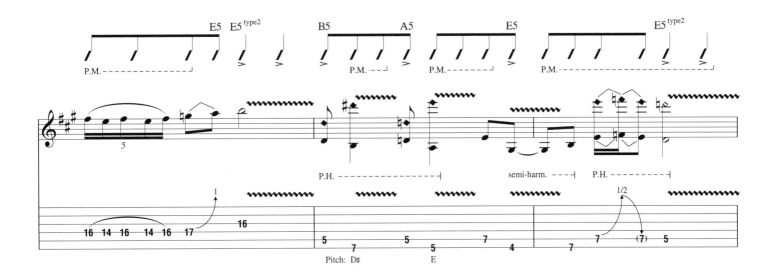

D.C. al Coda 2

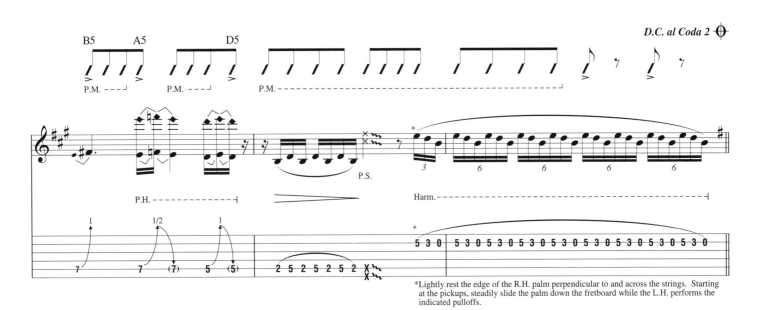

*Lightly rest the edge of the R.H. palm perpendicular to and across the strings. Starting at the pickups, steadily slide the palm down the fretboard while the L.H. performs the indicated pulloffs.

Coda 2

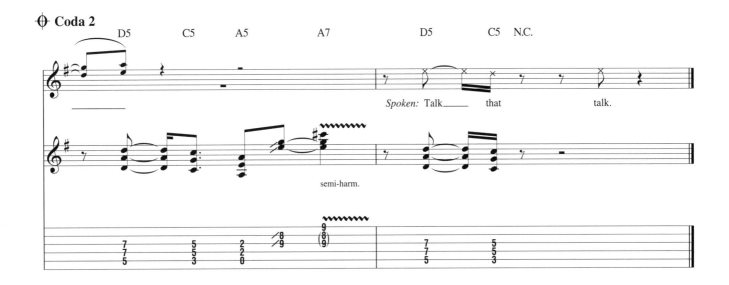

Spoken: Talk____ that____ talk.

No More Tears

Words and Music by Ozzy Osbourne, Zakk Wylde, Randy Castillo, Michael Inez and John Purdell

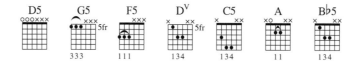

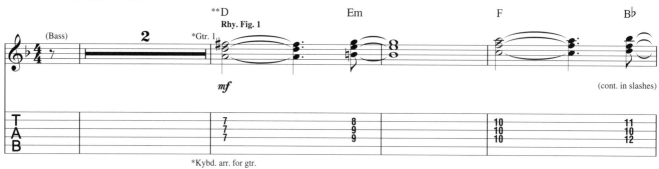

Drop D tuning, down 1/2 step:
(low to high) D♭-A♭-D♭-G♭-B♭-E♭

Intro

Moderate Rock ♩ = 104

*Kybd. arr. for gtr.

**Chord symbols reflect overall harmony.

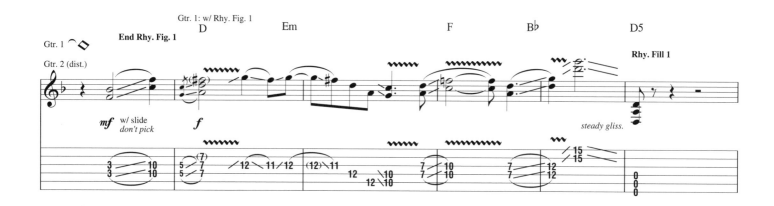

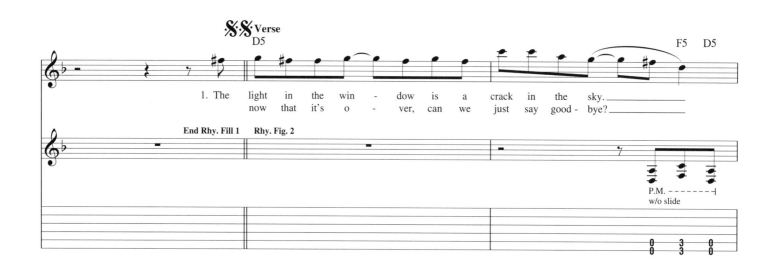

1. The light in the win - dow is a crack in the sky._____
   now that it's o - ver, can we just say good - bye?_____

Spoken: *He who laughs last, is just a hand in the bush.*

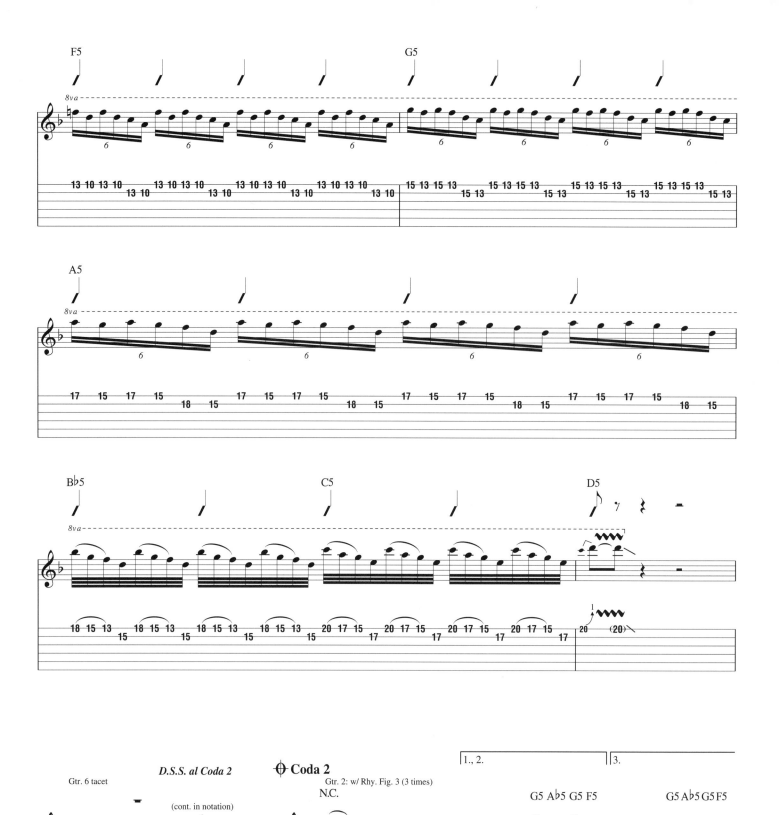

Mama, I'm Coming Home

Words and Music by Ozzy Osbourne and Zakk Wylde

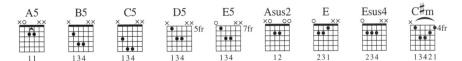

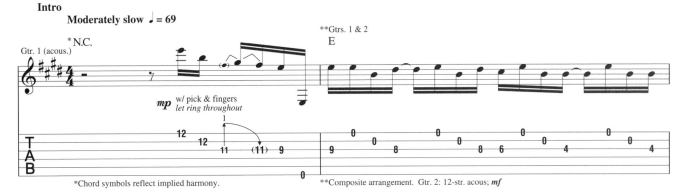

*Chord symbols reflect implied harmony.

**Composite arrangement. Gtr. 2: 12-str. acous; *mf*

1. Times have changed, and times are strange,

here I come, but I ain't the same. Ma-ma, I'm com-ing home.

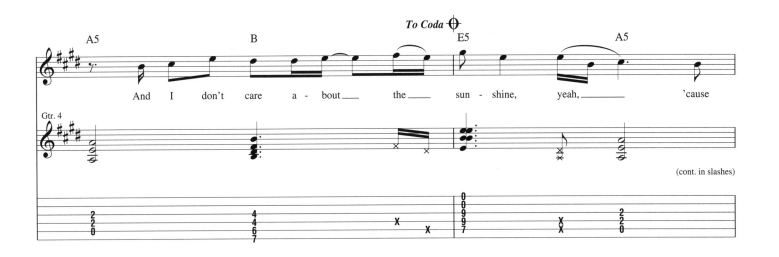

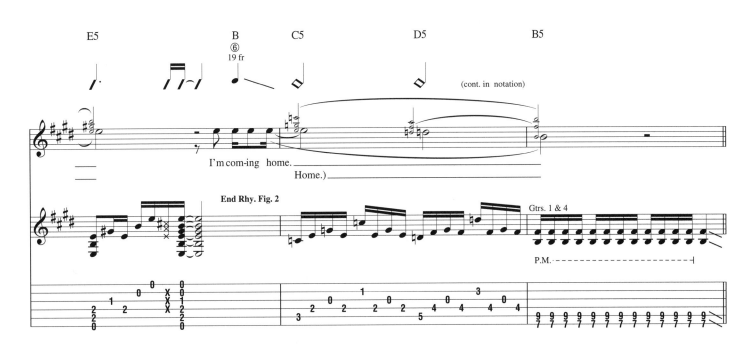

Interlude

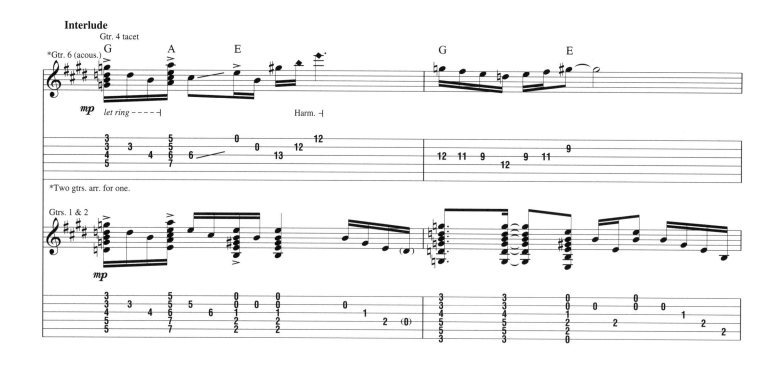

*Two gtrs. arr. for one.

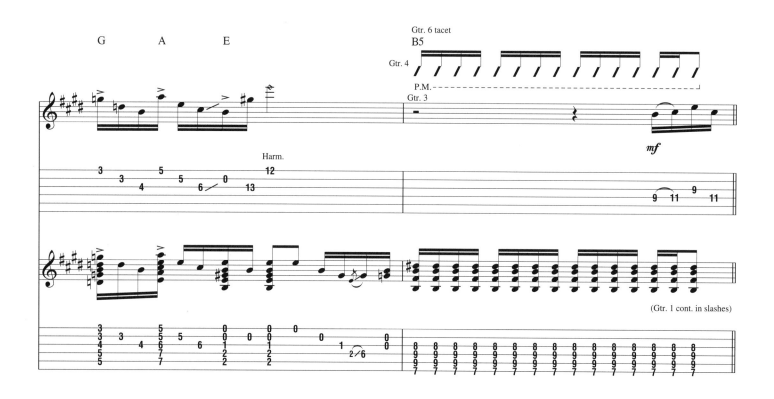

Guitar Solo

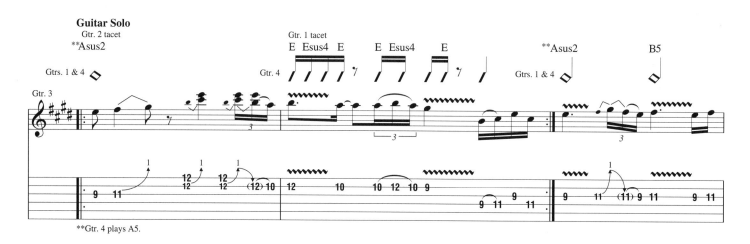

**Gtr. 4 plays A5.

I Don't Want to Change the World

Words and Music by Ozzy Osbourne, Zakk Wylde, Randy Castillo and Lemmy Kilmister

Tune down 1/2 step:
(low to high) E♭-A♭-D♭-G♭-B♭-E♭

Intro
Moderately fast Rock ♩ = 126

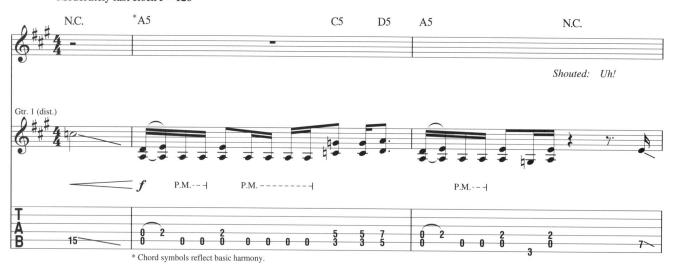

* Chord symbols reflect basic harmony.

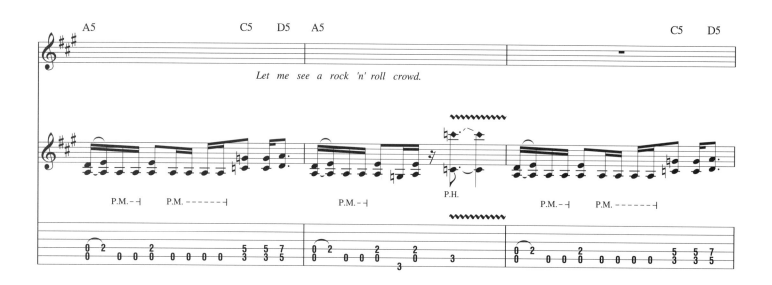

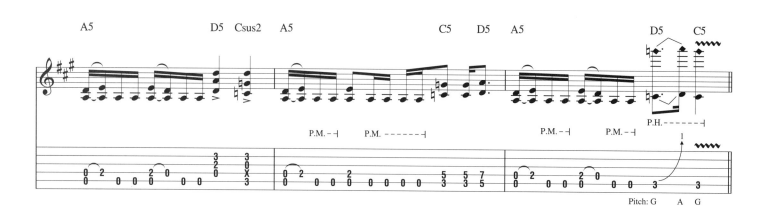

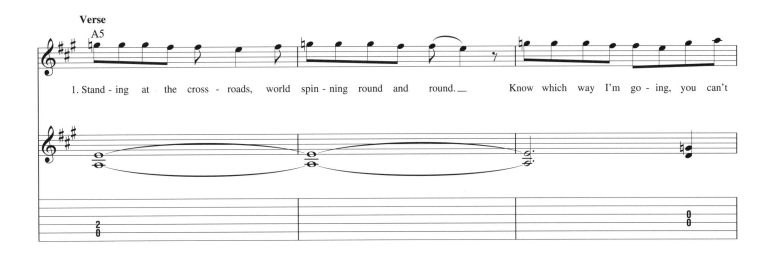

1. Stand-ing at the cross-roads, world spin-ning round and round.___ Know which way I'm go-ing, you can't

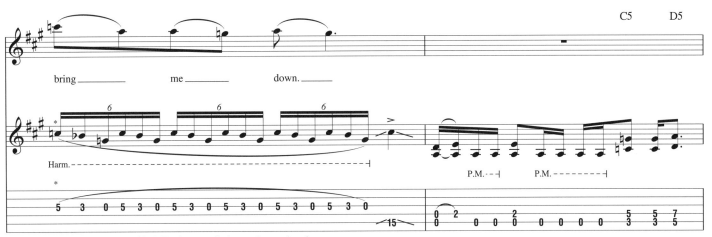

bring _____ me _____ down. _____

* Lightly rest the edge of the R.H. palm perpendicular to and across the strings.
  Starting at the pickups, steadily slide the palm down the fretboard while the L.H. performs the indicated pulloffs.

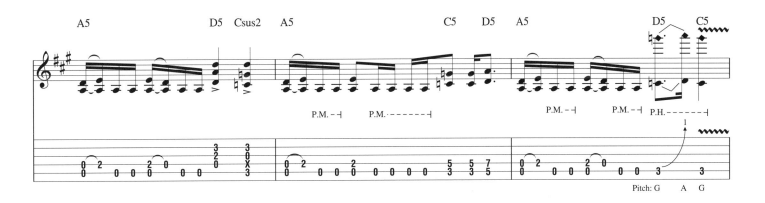

Pitch: G   A   G

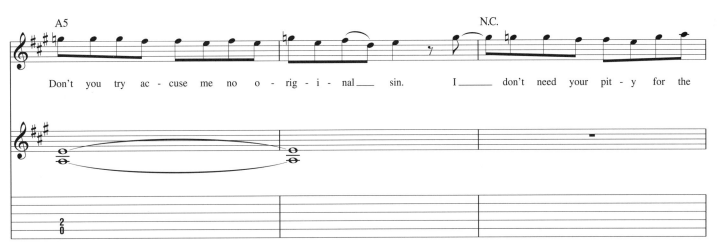

Don't you try ac-cuse me no o-rig-i-nal___ sin.   I ___ don't need your pit-y for the

* Bass plays A.

** sim.

*** Refers to harmonic only.

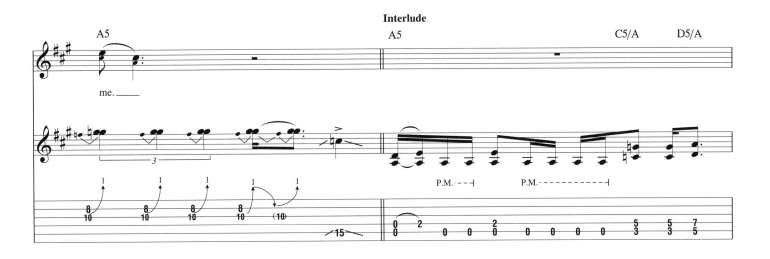

Interlude

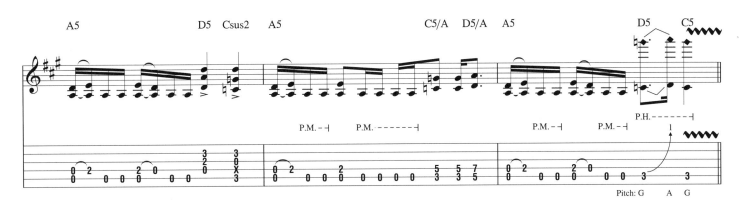

Verse

2. Tell me I'm a sin - ner, I got news _____ for _____ you, _____ I

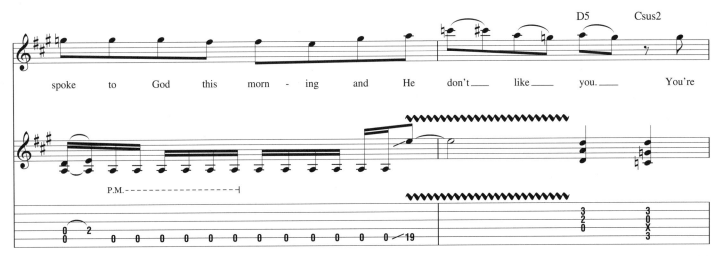

spoke to God this morn - ing and He don't _____ like _____ you. _____ You're

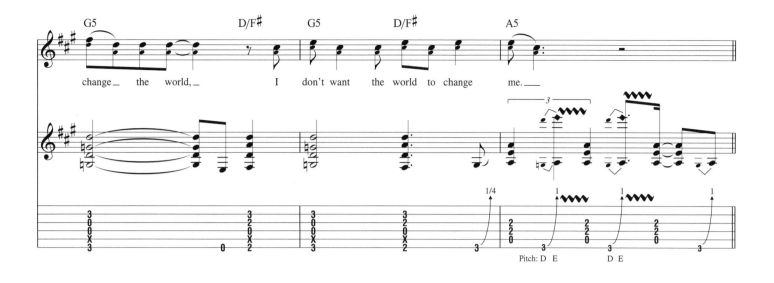

change the world, I don't want the world to change me.

Pitch: D E   D E

Bridge

You know it ain't eas-y.

Rhy. Fig. 2   End Rhy. Fig. 2

P.M.

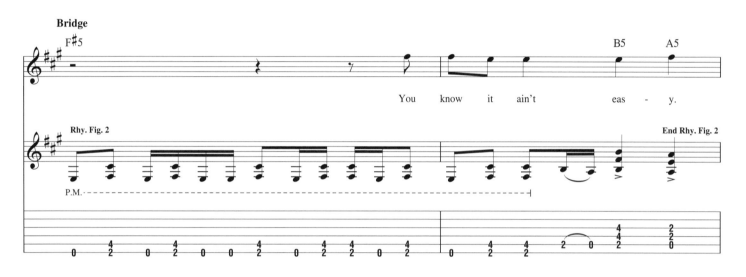

Gtr. 1: w/ Rhy. Fig. 2 (3 times)

You know it ain't fair. So

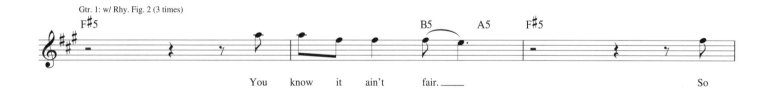

don't try and please me, be-cause I real-ly don't care.

Guitar Solo

Gtr. 1

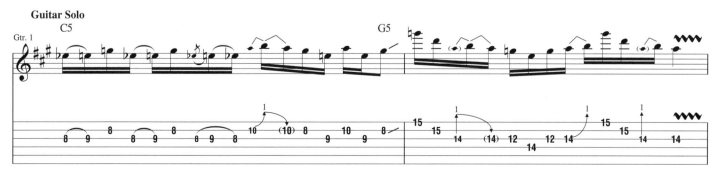

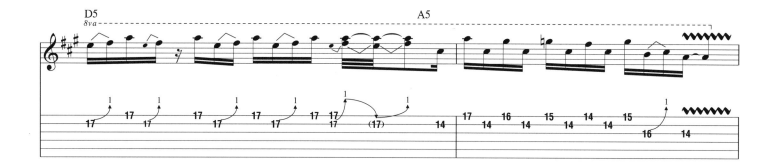

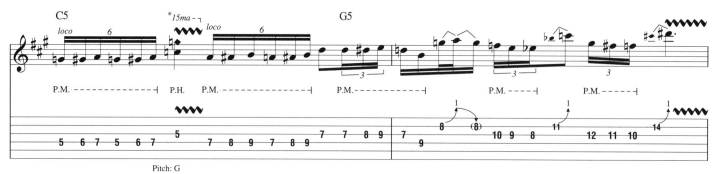

Pitch: G

* Refers to harmonic only

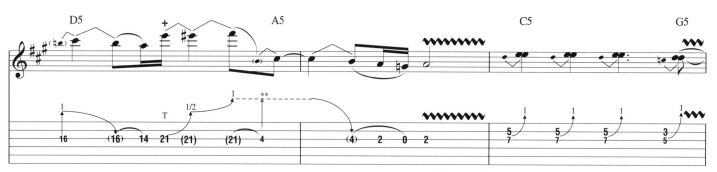

** Move L.H. down to the 4th fret while holding bend with R.H. finger.

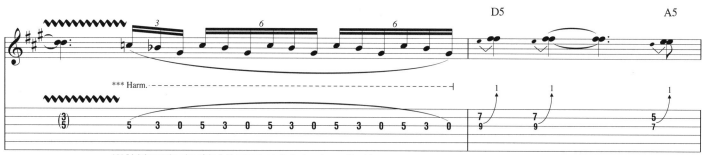

*** Lightly rest the edge of the R.H. palm perpendicular to and across the strings.
Starting at the pickups, steadily slide the palm down the fretboard while the L.H. performs the indicated pulloffs.

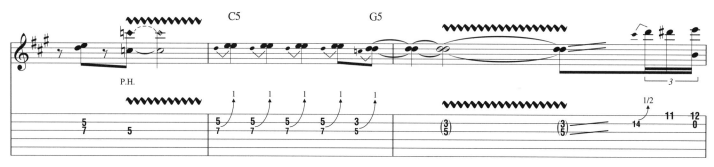

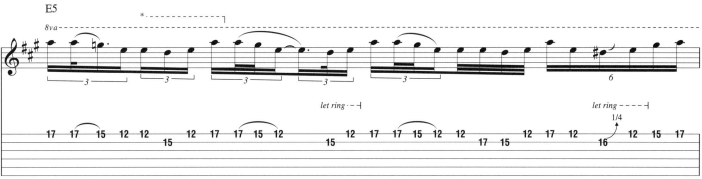

* Played behind the beat.

Bridge

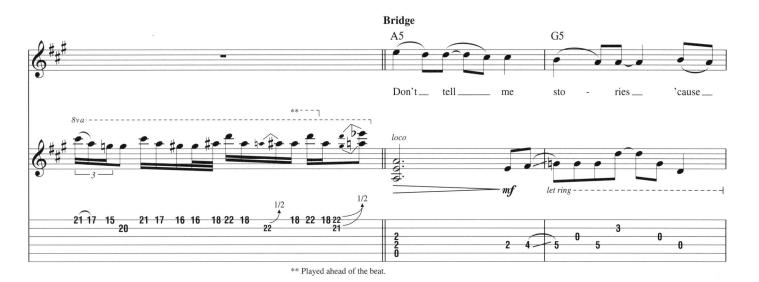

Don't tell me sto - ries 'cause

** Played ahead of the beat.

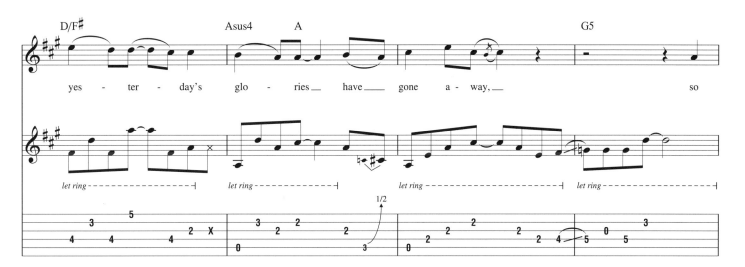

yes - ter - day's glo - ries have gone a - way, so

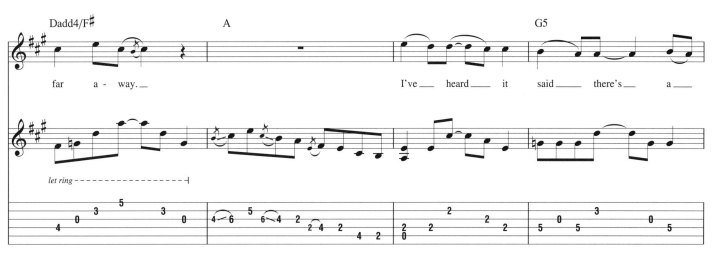

far a - way. I've heard it said there's a

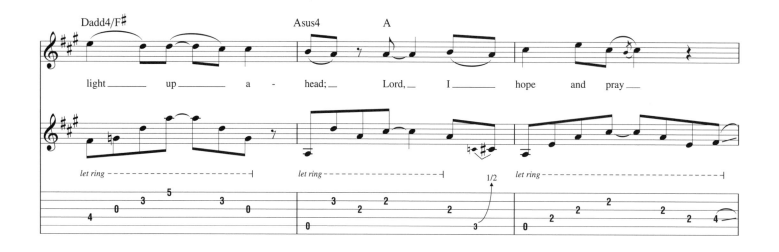

light _____ up _____ a - head; Lord, I _____ hope and pray _____

I'm here to stay, _____ yeah.

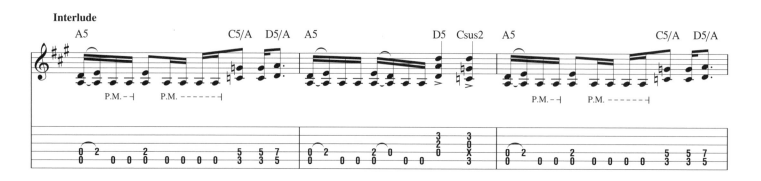

Interlude

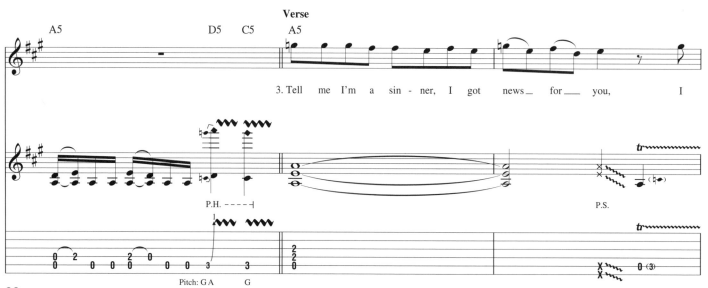

Verse

3. Tell me I'm a sin - ner, I got news _____ for _____ you, I

Pitch: G A   G

96

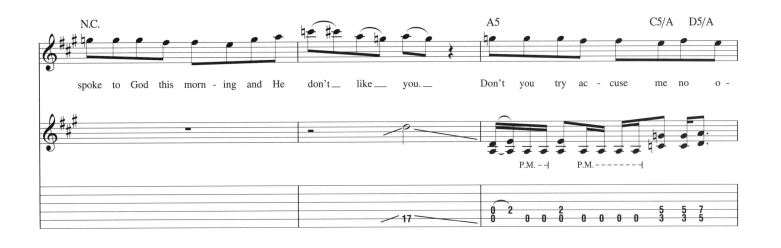

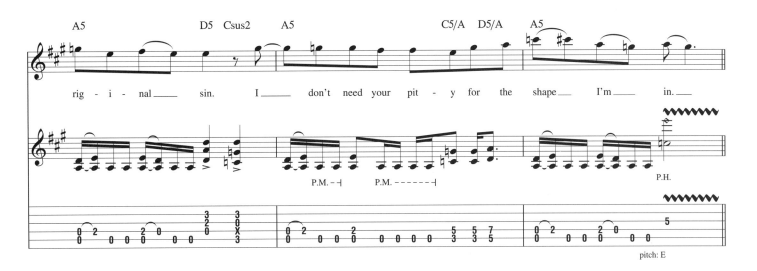

pitch: E

Chorus

Gtr. 1: w/ Rhy. Fig. 1 (1 1/2 times)

Gtr. 1

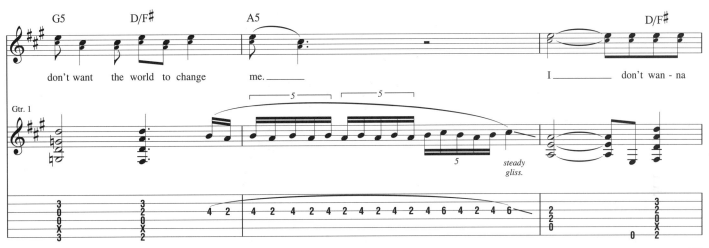

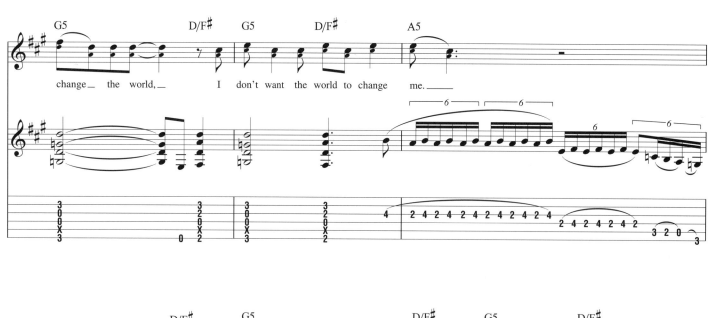

change_ the world,_ I don't want the world to change me._

I_____ don't wan - na change_ the world,_ I don't want the world to change

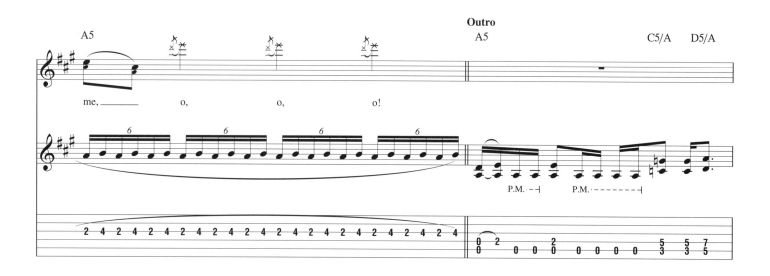

me,_ o, o, o!

Outro

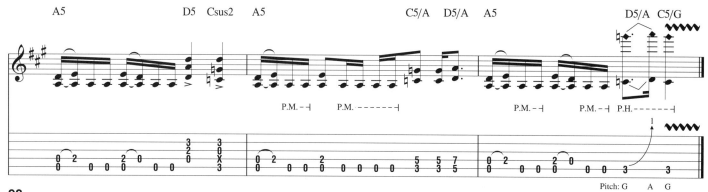

Pitch: G A G

I Just Want You

Words and Music by Ozzy Osbourne and Jim Vallance

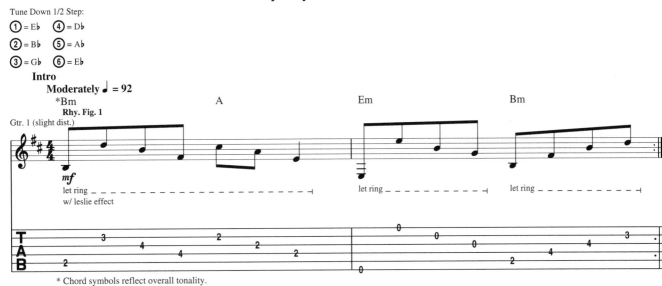

*Chord symbols reflect overall tonality.

Verse

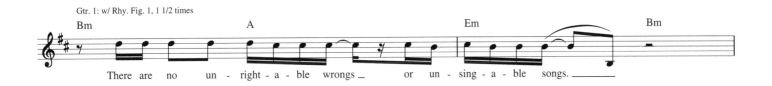

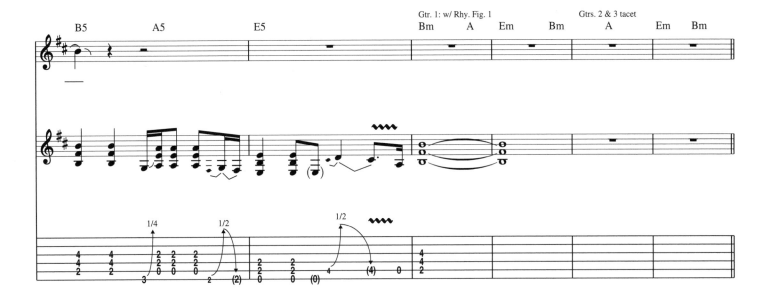

Verse

3. There are no un-crim-i-nal crimes, there are no un-rhym-a-ble rhymes.

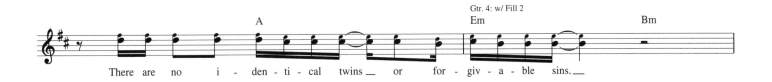

There are no i-den-ti-cal twins or for-giv-a-ble sins.

There are no in-cur-a-ble ills, there are no un-kill-a-ble thrills.

One thing and you know it's true. I don't ask much, I just want you.

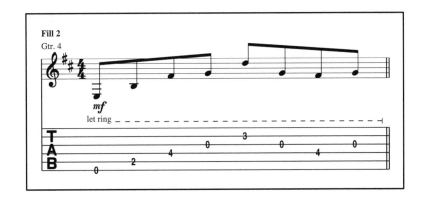

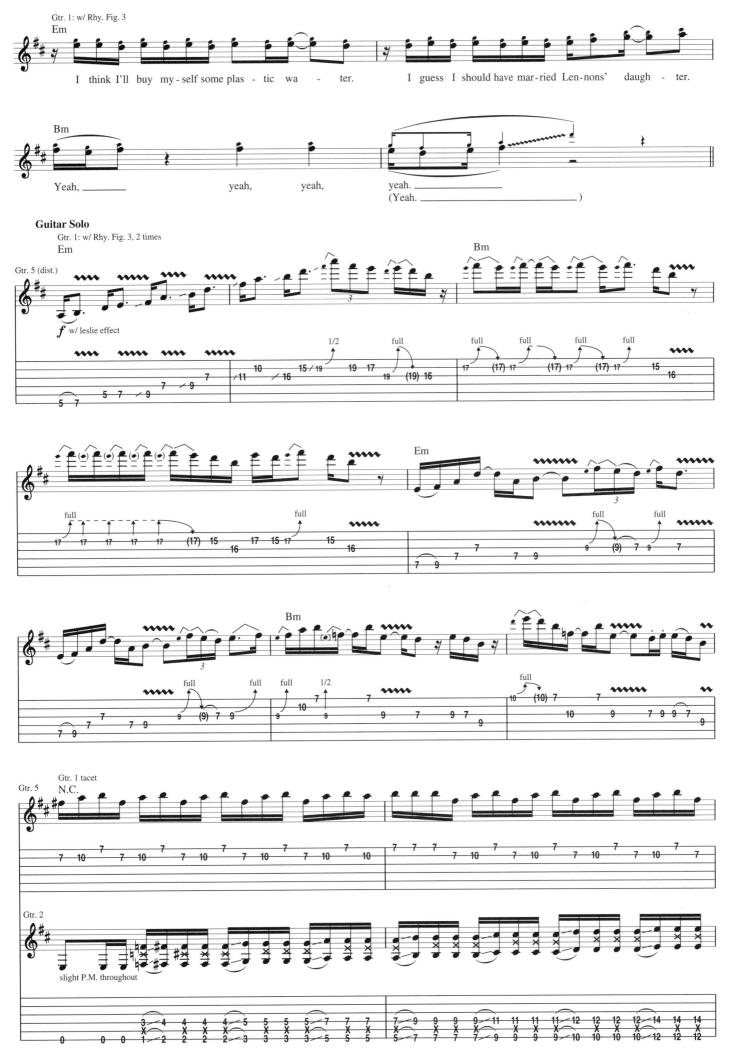

Verse
Gtrs. 2, 3 & 5 tacet

4. There are no un-a-chiev-a-ble goals,

let ring _ _ _ _ _ _ _ _ let ring _ _ _ _ _ _ _ _

Back on Earth

Words and Music by Richie Supa and Taylor Rhodes

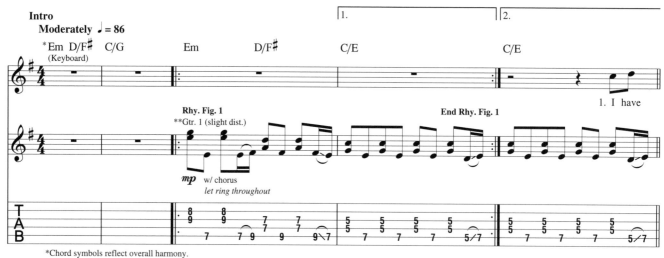

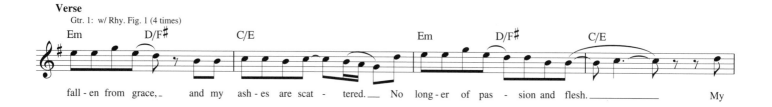

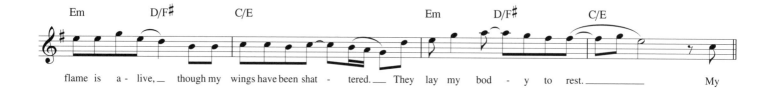

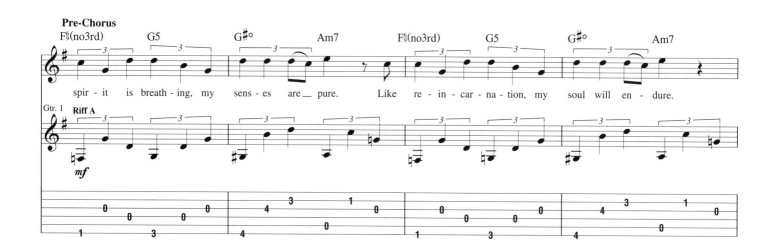

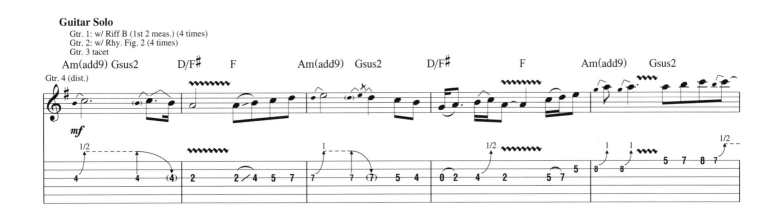

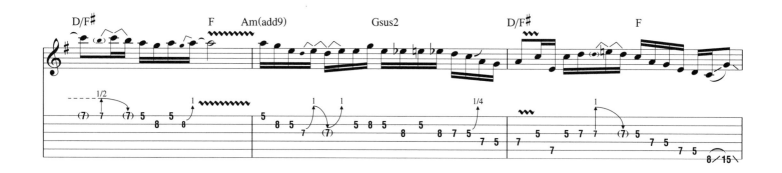

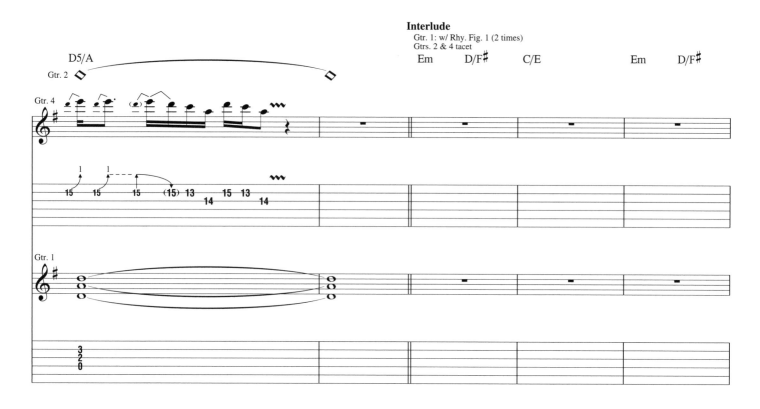

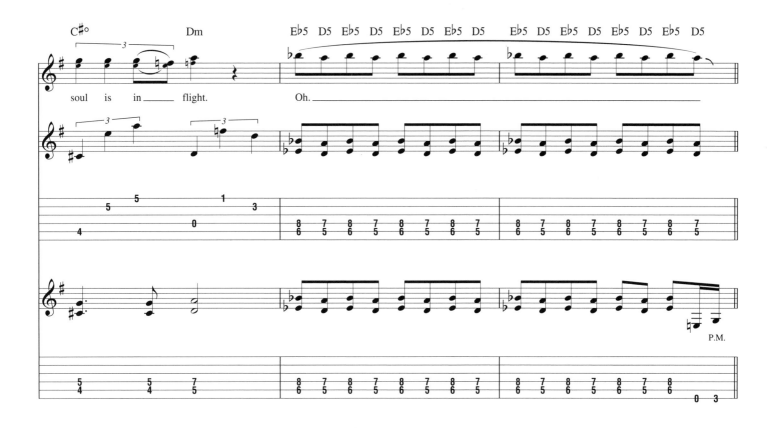

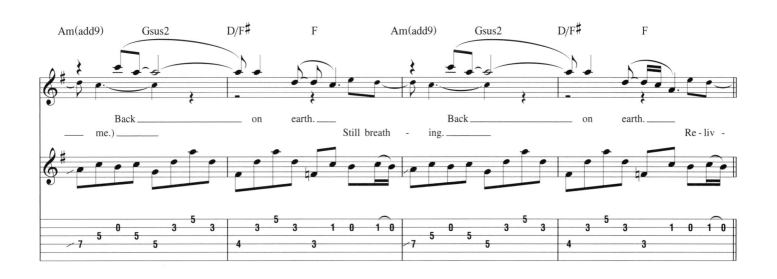

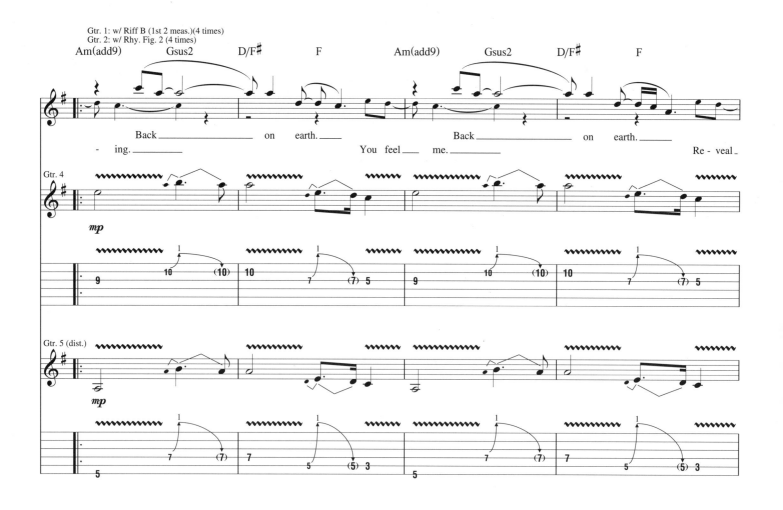

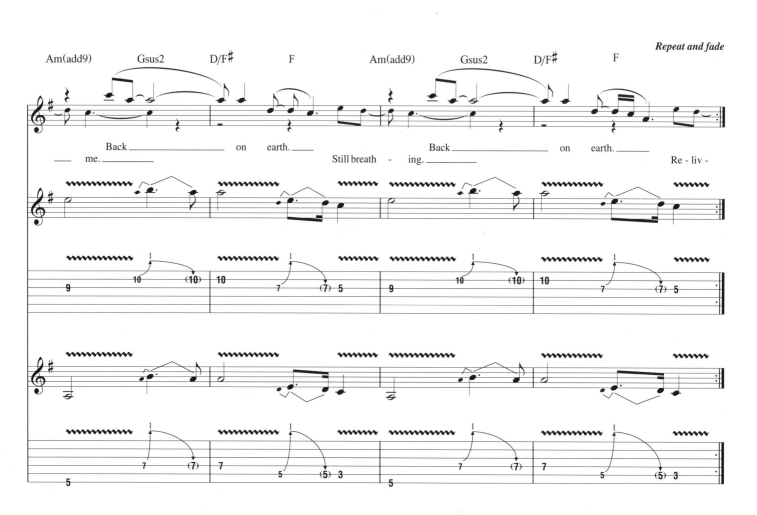